Seeing
Nature

Seeing Nature

Deliberate Encounters with the Visible World

PAUL KRAFEL

Chelsea Green Publishing Company
White River Junction, Vermont
Totnes, England

Designed by Dede Cummings Designs

Printed in the United States.
First printing, November 1999.

02 01 00 99   1 2 3 4 5

This book is printed on acid-free, recycled paper.

Library of Congress Cataloging-in-Publication Data

Krafel, Paul, 1950-
    Seeing Nature: deliberate encounters with the visible world
    / Paul Krafel.
            p.   cm.
    ISBN 1-890132-42-X (alk. paper)
    1.   Ecology—philosophy. 2. Philosophy of nature.
    3. Human ecology. I. Title.

    QH540.5 .K73 1999
    508 21—dc21   99-044945

Green Books Ltd
Foxhole, Dartington
Totnes, Devon TQ9 6EB United Kingdom
44-1-803-863-843

Chelsea Green Publishing Company
Post Office Box 428
White River Junction, VT 05001
(800) 639-4099
www.chelseagreen.com

For Alysia

who covered for me
when it rained.

Contents

Seeing
Nature

Ten Years Later—
Looking Back

ᘛᘚᘚᘓ

 OU HOLD THIS BOOK OF HOPE because many other readers, finding hope within it, passed it on. When I wrote this book, I knew it was too quiet and hard to categorize to be easily published. But part of the message I needed to share was: "Begin the work even though you cannot see the path by which this work can lead to your goal. Do not block your power with your current understanding." So I wrote the book, titled it *Shifting*, and self-published.

At the end of the book I wrote, "Working in the fields has taught me never to underestimate the power within upward spirals, because they create new allies that create unimagined possibilities. Faith that allies will emerge, for example, has led me to self-publish this book even though I have no way to distribute it. I am trusting in the power of readers to help it reach other readers. If this book has helped you see your world in delightful, uplifting ways, then please help the book by passing this copy on to a friend with your recommendation." I mailed copies to forty people who I thought might like the book.

Many of them bought copies to pass on to others who bought copies and passed them on. In this way, the quiet book quietly spread more than thirty-fold, until Barbara Damrosch passed it on to Chelsea Green Publishing Company. Chelsea Green scratched its company head. "This book doesn't fit into the established market niches. How will we ever market it?" But they believe the book is important and serves their mission. So they have added their gifts to this book. The most obvious changes are the graceful illustrations and the beautiful cover, but they have added an even greater, invisible power. Together, we have poured our love and dreams into a book that we hope shifts the way you see the world. If our offering touches you, please continue the tradition that brought it to you and pass it on.

May my stories nourish your visions of wonder and your works of hope.

Shifting Assumptions

The Mistake of the Sand Fleas

⌐

THE YOUNG CITY BOY had never been in a forest before; the possibility of seeing wildlife excited him. Each time he glimpsed a bird, he ran toward it, pointing exuberantly with his arms and shouting, "There's a bird! There's a bird!" Each bird flew away as he rushed it. Eventually the boy became frustrated. "It's not fair. Every time I see a bird, it flies away." I smiled. He was right. Every bird he saw did fly away. What he did not realize was that it was his response to seeing them, his running and shouting, that had scared them away. He didn't understand how he influenced the world that he saw. "He's young," I thought. "He'll learn."

⌐

Yet I do the same thing. My wife, Alysia, and I camped on the seashore for a week. Each time I walked to and from the ocean, I crossed the strand line of rotting seaweed that marked the high tide. There, each time, I saw countless sand fleas hopping randomly about. I figured that they must spend their lives hopping about, because that was all I ever saw them doing.

After several days of noticing their seemingly mindless behavior, I decided to stop long enough to see what one of these hoppers looked like. I sat down in their hopping midst and waited for one to land close enough and long enough for me to observe it. Within a minute, all the hopping had ceased. The sand fleas began going in and out of burrows and digging new ones. Two sand fleas joined together. "Mating," I thought, but then I noticed that they were joined mouth to mouth. The longer I watched, the more behaviors I saw.

I eventually stood up; the sand fleas all began hopping about again. Then I understood! Whenever a large, potential predator like me approaches, the fleas defend themselves by all hopping. The confusing appearance of this random hopping distracts the predator from focusing on one victim long enough to catch it. Everybody hopping protects everybody.

The reason I had seen the sand fleas always hopping whenever I approached them was because I was approaching them. I had mistakenly assumed that the only behavior I ever saw was the only behavior the sand fleas ever had.

⌒

Our culture can do the same thing. Our assumptions about nature are based on what we see around us but what we often see, especially from the cities that have dominated our culture for thousands of years, are the influences of our presence on the world. This can create false yet deeply rooted assumptions about nature. Because of these inaccurate assumptions, our actions often produce results we do not intend. The goal of this book is to shift these assumptions by describing a different way to understand the world.

This different way involves the Gaia Hypothesis, a scientific hypothesis about the Earth and its life formulated by James Lovelock and Lynn Margulis. Their hypothesis had such a profound effect upon me that it led me to a new work. That work and the lessons it taught me are the heart of this book; I describe them in the third section, Shifting Balances.

When I first read about the Gaia Hypothesis, I was struck by its obvious truth. I understood it because the hypothesis depends on seeing the world in a way that I had been practicing for years. After graduating from college, I had immersed myself in wilderness. Those wilderness years led to eight more years as a naturalist with the National Park Service. Climbing mountains, floating down rivers, roaming tundra and desert, watching deer decay, and sitting in silent cliff dwellings changed the way I saw the world. Learning this different way to see will help you understand the Gaia Hypothesis, so I share some of my vision-changing experiences in the second section, Tools for Seeing.

But first let me tell you some stories about cultural assumptions so you can better understand the goal of this book, which is to shift assumptions within our culture.

We Become What
We Practice

⤢

CULTURAL ASSUMPTIONS INFLUENCE the way we see the world. I became delightfully aware of such assumptions during the three summers that I led tours through cliff dwellings in the Southwest. The most frequent comment visitors made when they first entered the long-abandoned town was, "Look at the size of those doors. The people must have been tiny." Most of the doors are only two feet tall. The tallest doors are four feet. The stone buildings themselves are only four to five feet tall so the conclusion that the people were tiny seems logical. And yet the skeletons found near the town indicate a stature that is average for people in the world today: a few inches smaller than the average American, but definitely not tiny. What assumptions led our conclusion astray?

One assumption is that all of these buildings are homes. When we think of people living in a town, we think of our own neighborhoods. Almost all of the buildings in our own neighborhoods are houses or apartments. When we think of our neighborhoods with our houses and our pantries full of food, we often forget about the large buildings we enter every week to replenish our food supply. And hundreds of miles beyond our neighborhoods are huge buildings: food-processing factories, twenty-story grain elevators, and ten-million-bushel warehouses. The concentration of houses in our neighborhoods would be impossible without those remote buildings and the trucks and trains that link us to them. In the cliff dwelling, all of this is contained in one "town." The majority of buildings are not houses but "warehouses" in which were stored a year's supply of food for a hundred people.

This concentration of corn, squash, beans, and nuts had to be protected from mice. In fact, towns are impossible if people cannot solve the mice problem. Small doors are one solution. The smaller the opening, the more reliably one can completely seal off a room so that the food within will still be there if a drought withers next year's crop.

A second assumption of ours is that doors must be large enough to pass through easily. We live within many rooms. Doorways are something we pass through many times a day, so we build them large. But these rooms sit within a great stone alcove within a massive, sandstone cliff. The alcove itself forms a great stone room arching four hundred and fifty feet over the town.

During the hot days of the overhead summer sun, the alcove keeps the town in cool, pleasant shade. The low winter sun, however, shines into the alcove and warms the town. I've sat bareskinned in the town when snow lay in the canyon beyond. During a thunderstorm, a waterfall plunges in front of the alcove while the town remains completely dry behind it. Swifts and ravens circle and swoosh through the alcove. Canyon wrens forage within it, filling the town with their melodic glissades. The shape of the alcove focuses sound like a great ear. When I sit quietly, I can hear the spring trickling and birds scratching in the oak leaves a hundred yards away.

Why spend the day in small, smoke-blackened rooms when one lives within the alcove's incredible space? The people who lived here probably spent most of their time outdoors on top of the level roofs. What we see only as flat rooftops are also the level floors of the main living spaces. Most of the rooms were for food; the roofs were for people. People passed through doors only occasionally. The smoke-blackened living rooms were probably used only on colder winter nights. If the most important function of a living room is to hold a fire's heat against the freezing night outside, then a small door makes sense. A smaller door is easier to seal against the cold just as it is easier to seal against the mice.

⌣

Assumptions that are logical within our culture obscure our understanding of this other culture. What was it really like to be one of these people? This question surfaces each time I visit this place. Little things trigger reveries of thought and wonder—such as a piece of abalone shell.

It was just a fragment of the shell, smoothed into an ornamental shape with a hole drilled through it, perhaps part of a necklace. But abalone? Here in the arid canyon country of the Southwest? The Pacific Ocean is five hundred miles away with the Mojave Desert in between. Did a traveler bring it all the way to this town? Or was it passed from hand to hand, from culture to culture? Was a single abalone shell cut into smaller and smaller pieces and gradually dispersed over the Southwest? If so, what stories accompanied this shell and were fragmented along with it?

Have you played the game where a message is passed along a line of people and by the end, the message is completely different? Perhaps that happened as each giver of the shell passed on the story of this beautiful thing. How would a desert dweller pass on to another desert dweller stories of water stretching to the horizon? How would the ceaseless pounding of the surf be understood by people living near tiny, trickling springs? How would a beach—wet sand without trees—be understood in a region where wet sand always brings forth cottonwoods and willows? Surely these canyonlands created assumptions in the minds of their inhabitants.

According to anthropologists, these people were the descendants of a migration that left the Old World at least ten thousand years ago. That migration occurred before people in the Old World began agriculture, formed cities, developed the wheel, used metal, and evolved writing. The things that we associate with civilization developed after this migration of people left and settled North and South America. This migration of people went on to develop civilization in the New World but the most basic assumptions underlying their civilization might be different from ours.

One archaeologist, for example, wonders whether we use the wrong assumption when we label as "trade" the movement of materials between regions. In the Americas, it may have been gift-giving. Each region has resources that are scarce in other regions. Bringing these resources as gifts helps maintain an open hospitality to travelers. The resulting distribution of resources resembles trade, yet the assumptions and feelings underlying that distribution could have been very different.

Another archaeologist assumes that a stick across the doorway meant "No one home." How different a stick is from a steel deadbolt lock! How different might have been their sense of property. Most of our property is mass-produced and difficult to identify. Yet in a culture where each item is individually and uniquely crafted, the identity of the few pieces of property would be known by all. Stealing and trust would be different in this stone town.

Was the town noisy? Perhaps, with a hundred people living so closely together. On the other hand, the acoustics of the alcove carry sound so well that, within an hour, the people on my tours were talking much more quietly than normal. How loudly did the original inhabitants talk?

People on my tours sometimes noticed how straight the walls stood. "All their walls are so straight. They must have been good builders." That conclusion seemed simple and safe until one day I realized, "Not necessarily." Gravity is constantly pulling down on things. Walls that were not straight have fallen. The only walls remaining are the straight walls. We see a skewed sample. We see their building craft at its best.

Ancient corncobs lying about the ruin are only a few inches long. How was farming different when your corn was that small? Some archaeologists suggest that the most important crops were the deer, squirrels, and rabbits that the garden lured within range of the gardening hunters.

Skeletal remains indicate that the average life span of these people was about thirty-five years. Most of us live our lives assuming that death is far in the future. How is life different when you expect to live only thirty-five years? How would this affect childhood, learning, marriage? We prevent our children from even holding a job or voting until their late teens. What was the maturity level of their teenagers?

I came to appreciate these cliff dwellings for the perspective they gave me on my own mind and culture. They allowed me to detect a multitude of assumptions that had been unconscious before. Yet the more assumptions I uncovered, the more inaccessible these canyon dwellers became. Who were these people? I desired a more human bond than the animal basics of birth, food, and death.

⌒

Two stairways ascend the steep, rock slope to the stone village. The stairway that the tour follows goes straight up the slope. Its steps are two feet across and hewn deep into the stone. The gashes of steel chisels are fresh and easily visible. The National Park Service cut these steps so we could visit the town.

Off to the side is the almost invisible, original stairway into the town. The rounded steps are only a few inches deep. That is partly because they are worn down by use and time. Yet the steps are also only a few inches wide, wide enough for just one foot. In fact, the steps alternate: right, left, right, left. You have to start on the right foot to enter the town. This hand-and-toehold trail follows the flow of the rock, avoiding the steep areas, seeking the sections gradual enough not to need steps.

The cliff dwellers did not have metal. They had to pound with antler or harder rock. Carving a step was harder for them and required much more time. The step-makers minimized their labor by following the flow of the slope and carving only what was needed.

Some visitors could not climb even our broad, steel-carved steps. Almost all visitors, seeing the ancient stairs, thought climbing them was impossible, but the original dwellers, as children, would have seen the grown-ups going up and down the stairs. In fact, a baby might have gone up and down that hand-and-toehold trail on the back of a parent. A child would never have thought those stairs were impossible. Instead, those stairs posed a challenge. Solving that challenge gave a child the freedom to leave the town and explore the forested canyon beyond. Children would practice and look forward to the day when they could climb out of town just as our youth look forward to the day when they can drive out of the driveway.

In one cliff dwellings' plaza, where the women gathered to share their work, is a rock. It stands only two feet high with gently sloping sides. Any child could easily jump on top of it. Yet carved into the side are tiny hand-and-toeholds, closely spaced together—a playground for the crawlers and toddlers. Under the watchful eyes of the older generation, the babies practiced the skills they would need.

In the villages of the Hopis (the descendants of these people), I watch kids scramble up straight stone walls to get onto the roofs for a better view of the dances. If a child has to run all the way around the house to use the ladder, she won't get a front row seat. They will already be taken.

But stone steps are not part of our culture. There are no tiny hand-and-toehold trails in our playgrounds. Rock climbing is not required to leave our towns. And so when we encounter these steps, they seem impossible. Only wilderness travelers know how easy those steps really are—at least for those who practice walking on steep rock.

On the other hand, those canyon dwellers probably would have found it impossible to handle a world rushing toward them at fifty-five miles per hour. To us, it seems natural, because we have been practicing ever since we were driven home as newborns from the hospital delivery room. But my mother once drove around town with a man who had been in prison for years. He grew nervous when she drove more than twenty-five miles per hour. The world was moving too fast. He was out of practice.

The stone steps taught me that we become what we practice. The skills we practice with our bodies and the assumptions we practice in our minds shape us. Practice allows humans to create different cultures for different environments and different times. Practice allows humans to diverge. These canyon dwellers and I share the ability to adapt to different environments. The maze of assumptions separating me from those people is actually my most human bond with them.

Living Within
the Unknown

ONE EVENING I SAW THE EARTH TURNING. Before
that night, I had always seen the Sun setting toward a stationary horizon. But when I saw the Sun, instead, as stationary, then I saw my
horizon rising toward the Sun. In the first view, the Sun moves. In the
second view, my world moves. My eyes see the same thing—the gap
between Sun and horizon closing. Yet what is moving? My mind must
make an assumption. Shifting that assumption changes the world I see.

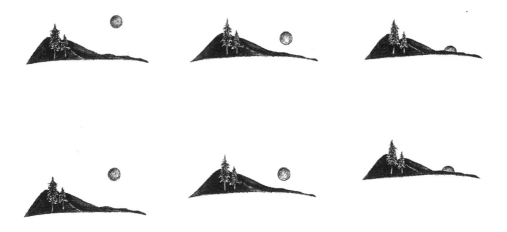

I can see the sun as setting . . . or the horizon as rising.

I tried to teach my new view of the "sunset" to two young boys, but they already saw the Earth rolling us away from the Sun, tipping us backward. The boys liked to exaggerate the effect by falling backward as they watched their horizon tilt up in front of the Sun.

Maybe when I was a child, I also saw the Earth turning, tipping me back. But the word "sunset" channeled my perception and I began to see the Sun moving down rather than myself spinning away. We become what we practice and I began to practice living on an unmoving, passive world with change happening "out there" beyond my world.

During most of the "sunsets" of my life, I have watched only the spectacular colors above the western horizon. However, this sense of "falling backward" made me turn around to see what I was falling into. In the pink eastern sky, a purple duskiness rises above the horizon soon after sunset. This darker purple is the shadow of the Earth streaming out through the atmosphere. I had never noticed that the Earth, like any object in sunlight, casts a shadow. The shadow "rises" above the eastern horizon at the same rate as the Sun "sets" below the western horizon. Sometimes, depending on atmospheric conditions and my location, the shadow is easily visible as a purplish band of shade cutting through the atmosphere in the east. Other times, the shadow is subtle, marked simply by shaded clouds within the shadow and sunlit clouds above. (The Earth's shadow is most reliably seen at dawn, "sinking" toward the western horizon just before sunrise).

Sunset is the moment I am spun into the shadow. The trees, tall buildings, or mountains above me still shine in the golden sunlight because they rise above the shadow, yet they too will soon descend into it. The sky above me is also turning into the shadow but since the atmosphere floats upward for miles, its passage into night will take a long time.

Our thick atmosphere scatters much of the sunlight passing through it. This scattered light forms a shining fog of blue light, which we see as blue sky. (On the Moon, which has no atmosphere, the daytime sky is as black as night.) The lower atmosphere loses this blue shine as it passes into shadow. The upper atmosphere still floats in the sunlight overhead but the upper atmosphere is less dense and reflects only a tiny fraction of the sunlight that streams through it. The sky's shining blue of day recedes to a more distant, glowing blue, thin enough to see through to the stars.

Eventually, all of the atmosphere above me turns into the shadow. Sunlight still streams by overhead but it passes hundreds of miles above the atmosphere, so none of it is reflected down to my eyes. The blue fog of day clears and I can see the eternal blackness of space.

Watching the atmosphere change as it descends into the shadow makes night more than a time. Night is a place. Night is a journey. Night is a slow, spinning passage through a shadow that is always streaming directly away from the Sun. Sunrise is our emergence from the other side of the shadow. Change is happening beneath my very feet. Space is not "out there"; I live within space.

How would our culture change if we practiced watching our Earth turn so that each "sunrise" and "sunset" reminded us daily that we live on a spinning, round, and therefore finite world? We need better words for "sunset" and "sunrise." If more accurate, beautiful words come to your mind, please tell me.

⌒

A shift in another visual assumption profoundly changed our culture four hundred years ago. Before that shift, Europeans actually saw a universe different from the modern universe because they believed that the Sun and stars circled the Earth.

That belief had a problem, though. How could all those circling stars stay in formation? The stars appear to move at different speeds across the night sky (with the North Star not moving at all), and yet the six thousand visible stars remain in the same familiar constellations over thousands of years. How could that be if each star circled the Earth independently?

There was only one possible explanation: The Earth must be standing immovably at the exact center of an immense, rotating, star-encrusted celestial sphere containing the entire universe.

How big was that "universe"? Its size was limited by the fact that it must be able to rotate once every day (*universe* means "one turn" in Latin). The farther away the edge of the universe, the faster the celestial sphere had to spin. Think of a clock's second hand: Although all parts of the second hand make a complete turn each minute, the outer tip of the second hand must travel much farther than the inner part. Therefore, the outer tip must move much faster than the inner part. This is true of any turning thing. The outer edge of a merry-go-round moves much faster than the inner part. The outermost child in crack-the-whip is hurled around the playground. And the farther the stars are from the Earth (which stands at the center of the celestial sphere), the faster those stars must move in order to complete one turn in twenty-four hours.

If the stars were ten thousand miles away, for example, the celestial sphere would have to carry them around at more than 2,500 miles per hour in order to complete a turn in twenty-four hours. If the stars were a million miles away, the celestial sphere would have to spin more than 250,000 miles per hour. If all the stars were as close as our Sun (almost 100 million miles), the outer edge of the celestial sphere would have to hurtle around at almost 25 million miles per hour.

So the size of the universe depended on each person's image of how fast the stars moved. This was in a time when some of the fastest things known were horses and arrows. If you were a crazy adolescent, maybe you could imagine stars moving a thousand miles per hour and therefore you could live in a universe in which the stars were almost four thousand miles away. But if you were a conservative old fuddy-duddy . . . well, the celestial sphere was the noble container of the universe. It should behave in a dignified manner. It should turn sedately, not whirl about crazily. For you, maybe the stars serenely moved only ten miles per hour, in which case they were only forty miles away.

Four hundred years ago, people lived at the center of a tiny universe. If the Sun and Moon were only a few miles away, then obviously they were small objects. The only large object in the entire universe was the Earth. That explained why the Earth stood at the center while everything else circled around it. One's sense of God and history would be very different within that universe.

Now imagine you are a European of four hundred years ago who has heard rumors of a new idea, rumors that the stars do not revolve around the Earth, that the celestial sphere does not exist. You go out under the stars to consider these ideas. You know the stars well, for they are your calendar and nighttime clock. You know them far better than Americans will know them four hundred years later because no television holds you inside at night. No electric lights or car roofs obscure the stars when you journey out at night. No moving airplane lights or satellites distract you from the slower pace of the turning stars. You stand at the center of your familiar universe, looking up at the well-known, nearby stars, when suddenly—it can happen no other way—the celestial sphere shatters and the stars are hurled to varying, unknown distances.

This shattering of the universe will profoundly change the culture—and yet visually the only change was a shift in assumptions. The image of a celestial sphere created the assumption that all stars were the same distance from the Earth. If all the stars were at the same distance, then every variation in star brightness was due to variations in star size. This created the visual assumption that brighter stars were larger stars and fainter stars were smaller stars.

However, if the celestial sphere does not exist and stars are not all the same distance away, then perhaps all the stars are the same size and the variations we see in brightness are due to variations in distance. Suddenly, the brightest stars become the closest stars. Faint stars, which had been easily overlooked in the previous view, now draw the mind out farther and farther. Where the equidistant boundaries of the universe reassuringly stood a few seconds ago, a gaping universe suddenly engulfs you. Suddenly, the Sun, the Moon, and the stars are of unknown size. If the faintest stars are the farthest away, can there be other stars so far away that they can't be seen? The darkness between stars fills with unknown possibilities. Is this universe too big to see?

That vision probably made some Europeans sink to their knees, sick to their souls. Many people desperately leaped back to their old way of seeing, rejecting the new heresy. But for a second, they had seen a different universe and their old universe would never be as self-contained as it had been before. Night after night, person by person, more people saw the new universe and as they practiced that vision, they became a new culture.

⌐⌐

I like to practice that shift. Even though I know that the apparent brightness of stars is actually a result of both their distance and intrinsic brightness, I like to gaze at the stars and pretend that all the stars are at the same distance. I see variations in brightness as variations in the size of the stars. The sky appears uniformly "flat." My attention focuses on the few, bright, important stars. The darkness between stars is blank space. Then I shift my assumption; I assume all the stars have the same intrinsic brightness and I see variations in brightness as variations in distance. Space becomes very three dimensional. The faint stars (there are so many of them) draw my attention out to the edge of my vision. Just as I see more trees or buildings (though smaller) in the distance than close at hand, so I see more faint stars because there is vaster volumes of space farther out than "close at hand." The darkness between stars fills with mystery. Forty-three of the fifty closest stars, for example, are too faint for us to see. The universe stretches far into the darkness.

In both views, my eyes see the same points of light but my mind sees completely different universes. The sudden transformation is breathtaking and yet I will never even come close to feeling that shift the way those Europeans felt it, because I can never imagine stars as close and small as they could. For those Europeans, that shift shattered their universe. For me, it shatters my complacency. Growing up in the Space Age, I had assumed that the unknown lay Out There, securely removed beyond the known world around me. I had assumed that I saw the world the way it really is. Yet if shifting a simple visual assumption can suddenly reveal a new universe or reveal a world spinning me into its shadow, then what other surprises fill this "known" world, hiding behind unconscious assumptions at this very moment? Perhaps any part of my world might change at any time. I live within the unknown.

⸰

A new scientific "rumor" is now circulating through our culture, a rumor that the world works differently than we've thought. The Gaia Hypothesis will alter our vision of our Earth as profoundly as the shifting stars altered the Europeans' vision of their universe. This book describes the new vision in enough detail that you can experience it. My description, however, requires the tools of a naturalist. Since these are not used much in our urban culture, I will present them first.

Tools

for

Seeing

The Fit

⌐⌐

I walked from my car to a spectacular canyon overlook. Leaning over the rail, I looked down hundreds of feet to the river. The canyon cried out for a rock to be thrown over its edge. I looked around for a rock but there were none; all the rocks had already been thrown over that edge. Since watching a rock arc and accelerate into that abyss was worth a bit of a walk, I went searching. The rocky desert had been picked clean. I searched farther and farther. Occasionally I would look back at the receding overlook, consider the distance, and decide that throwing a rock over the edge was still worth the walk back. I continued searching, amazed at how thoroughly the area had been picked clean of rocks. Finally, I walked so far away that when I looked back at the overlook, I said, "Forget it." Throwing a rock was no longer worth the time and effort required to return to the overlook.

Three or four steps after that decision I saw rocks on the ground.

I stopped. Not to wonder whether I should go back; I had firmly rejected that choice. Rather, I stopped in delight at the Fit between my inner decision and those rocks. The shift from an absence of rocks to a presence of rocks was logically connected with my mental shift from "I will pick up any rock I find" to "I will leave behind any rock I find." The decisions of previous visitors had created a boundary between rocks and no-rocks and this boundary now made me conscious of the same decision within myself. My thought patterns fit with those of previous visitors. We all had decided that rocks at this distance just were not worth carrying all the way back to that overlook. We had constructed with rocks a scientific graph of how a mental compulsion fades with increasing distance.

During another day in another desert, I was peeing on a rock. Not much was moving in the afternoon heat. The biggest movement was my urine flowing across the surface of the rock, so I watched that. It converged into little streams that flowed over the edges of the rock onto the plants below. Plants were not common in this desert, so I thought it strange that my urine should be dropping onto plants. Then I saw the Fit. The slopes and cracks that guide my urine to those plants will also guide the rare rains to them. The rain falling on several square feet of rock will be channeled to a few square inches of desert soil. This concentration of moisture lavishly nourishes any desert seed lucky enough to drift to this spot.

I looked around at other rocks. They all had clumps of plants scattered around their bases. Above each clump was the end of a micro-valley draining the micro-slopes above it. A minute ago I had simply seen "rocks," a quick label that glossed over details. Now the Fit between rocks and plants drew my eyes to micro-drainages.

The micro-drainages were different sizes, which led me to notice that the clumps of plants were also different sizes. The larger micro-drainages had larger clumps of plants below them. The more runoff the clump received, the larger it could grow. This implies that all these clumps would expand during a wet year and contract during a dry year. Each clump was a rain gauge if I only knew how to read it.

I delight each time I discover the Fit between two pieces of the world. The delight is similar to (but deeper than) fitting together two pieces of a jigsaw puzzle. When two puzzle pieces fit together, they reveal more of the picture than they did apart. The delight I feel each time I see the Fit between pieces of the world feels like a glimpse of a beautiful picture too vast for me yet to see. Each glimpse tantalizes me to discover the Fit between other pieces.

The glint of a leaf fluttering down from an oak tree caught my eye. As the leaf drifted over a sunlit meadow, it began to rise. It must have drifted into a thermal, an upward surge of warm air heated by the sun-warmed ground of the open meadow. The glinting leaf rose almost out of sight. Then it floated over the tall pine trees bordering the meadow. The leaf quickly dropped into the trees. The abrupt descent told me of the shaded cool ground beneath the trees. No warm air rose from beneath those trees to uplift a leaf.

The Fit between the leaf's journey and the temperature of the ground beneath it revealed the invisible cycling of air between the warm meadow and the cool forest. Each example of Fit can expand my awareness because the visible often reveals an invisible piece with which it fits.

I sat resting beneath a bush on top of a brushy ridge. Once or twice a minute, a bird skimmed over the bush above me. Every bird in this intermittent flow passed within inches of my head and then dropped down

The stream of birds revealed where I was sitting—on the lowest point along the ridge.

the other side of the ridge. Why was this? I stood up to look around, and realized I was sitting in a pass. The birds want to conserve their energy when they fly over a ridge, so they cross it at the lowest point possible. The top of my bush happened to be this lowest point. The flights of birds fit with their landscape.

I have encountered the same thing with animal trails. When I left human trails to hike cross-country, I discovered that trails of other animals cover the world. Animals pass over the land every day and their feet create trails. Like birds, the animals cross a ridge at its easiest point. When I need to cross a ridge, I follow animal trails, trusting them to lead me along the path of least effort.

In Alaska, I followed the trails of mountain sheep along the ridges. Not all ridges are smooth and gently continuous. Rocky crags stick out of some ridges like teeth out of rotting gums. If I cannot see past the crag ahead of me, I do not know whether I should go to the right, to the left, or climb over the crag. In the beginning, I tried to decide, but I soon learned to simply follow the trail of the sheep. Sometimes their path goes easily over the crag, but usually the path leaves the ridge top. I follow, knowing the trail will skirt the crag and return me with the least effort to the ridge top. These trails are wise.

When these trails leave the ridge top and cut across a slope, however, they sometimes sag where they obviously should go straight. I must follow these sagging trails down and then laboriously back up. Walking straight across the slope seems like it would be easier but if I try shortcutting the sag, I find myself slipping downslope in loose gravel. The trail's compacted gravel makes easier walking even if the trail does sag inefficiently.

A series of trail remnants are always found downslope of these sagging sections. The farther a remnant is down the slope, the more faded it is, until the lowermost one fades back into the slope. It makes sense that the remnants down there are fading; nobody walks on them anymore. Their pattern of fading tells me that the lower the remnant, the longer it has been abandoned. This pattern of successive abandonments reveals that this section of slope is slowly sliding downhill. Those remnants used to be part of this trail up here but the sliding slope carried them down there.

The sagging section of trail on which I walk will someday be fading away down there. Eventually the sliding slope will carry this section of trail so far out of line that the sheep will abandon it. They will cut straight across the sliding slope and create a new trail upslope of this trail. Yet, over time, the sliding slope will carry that new trail (as well as the trails below) downslope. Eventually the new trail will sag too much. The sheep will abandon it and create a newer trail.

Seeing how the sheep shortcut these sagging trail sections led me to imagine a First Animal walking this ridge, not knowing the best route. The First Animal made many false detours, had to double back, and chose routes that were too long. Yet its passage created the first impression of a trail. Now those that follow can see the line of a trail ahead.

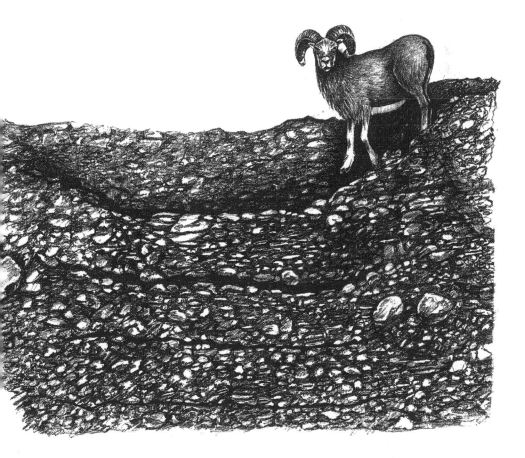

The sheep change the trail to fit the ever-changing slope.

They can observe possibilities for shortcuts and begin a shorter trail. Other animals coming to this fork in the trail will look ahead and choose the shorter trail. The abandoned trail fades under sliding gravel while the shorter, wiser trail grows more definite. This happens all along the trail until it passes over rugged land with elegant, knowledgeable grace. I follow such a trail confidently, knowing that it will lead me well.

These trails possess wisdom because they fit the ridge. Although the slopes slide and the trails sag, the path of least effort across each slope will be maintained. The sheep adjust the trail to maintain the Fit with the ever-changing slope. This Fit allows both the path and the sheep to survive.

I once interpreted "the survival of the fit" using "fit" as an adjective that described the kind of life that survives: strong animals, well-camou-flaged animals, or intelligent animals. Now I think of "fit" as a noun. The survival of the Fit. Both life and its environment might change but the Fit between them will survive.

Seeing Animals
as Individuals

⤴

*T*HERE IS NOT A LOT OF TRAFFIC on the back roads of the Yukon Territory so hitching a ride can take awhile. On the morning of the second day of waiting in a remote place, I was propped against my pack, taking a nap. I drowsily awoke. My tentatively opening eyes saw a red fox sitting twenty yards away on the road, attentively observing this strange sight of a man sleeping beside the road. As I became aware of what I was seeing, my head lifted, signaling that the show was over. The fox arose and trotted off the road into the forest.

Suddenly the fox froze. For several seconds, I had no idea why he had stopped. Then, down from a spruce tree fifty feet beyond the fox came a red squirrel, moving and chattering in a carefree way. When the squirrel reached the ground, it stood up on its hind legs, looked around briefly, then hopped a few feet toward the fox. Again it would stop, scrape and sniff about in the moss, look around, hop again, falsely secure. Hop by hop it moved closer to the fox. All this time, the fox maintained his frozen position but his energy grew more and more charged. He was trembling from the effort of not moving. His attention was focused completely on that squirrel. I could almost hear the fox thinking, "Keep coming. Keep coming. A little farther now." And the squirrel did. The fox quivered with anticipation but he did not move.

The fox was waiting, maintaining a decision not to spring. An invisible line lay somewhere between the fox and the squirrel. As long as the squirrel remained beyond that line, the squirrel would have the advantage in a chase back to its tree. But if the squirrel crossed the line, the advantage would shift to the fox. That shifting point is different for every hunted squirrel and every hunting fox. The more precisely a fox can gauge that line, the more successful that fox will be. Springing too soon is a mistake, but waiting too long is also a mistake. The squirrel might start hopping in the other direction. A bird's warning call or an unpredictable shift in the wind might destroy the advantage of surprise. This squirrel, however, seemed oblivious to the fox as it poked about in the forest floor. It hopped closer.

The fox sprang forward. The carefree squirrel became a terrified animal making its last desperate streak. The safety of the spruce tree drew the squirrel back and up into its branches like a released rubber band. The fox was right there at the tree but now the squirrel was in the branches chattering loudly. The fox gazed up at it for a few seconds. Then he turned back to me as if he had been conscious of my presence the entire time. He had the most embarrassed expression, as if to say, "You still watching? I really wish you hadn't seen that." He walked off into the forest.

⌒

The lovely song of the canyon wren begins as a melodious rush of notes down the major scale. This musical cascade gradually slows until it glides to a graceful stop at the bottom. I heard a young wren practicing this song. The young bird knew how to go down the scale but he had not yet learned how to slow down. His song plummeted like a rock until it hit the bottom of his vocal range, where it bounced around and died. Time and again, this adolescent launched himself into the song and crashed at the bottom with no perceptible sign of slowing. After each disaster he would be silent. Suspense. Would the bird give up? Again he began the song. Would he pull out of the dive this time? Again the song slid out of control, ending in sputtering attempts to reach a lower note.

I laughed at the poor fit between his attempts and the mature song of his species. Memories of adolescent awkwardness united me with that bird. Differences between species are so obvious that I often overlook our similarities. For all of us, the Fit is not guaranteed at birth. The potential is there, but the precision is not. For all of us, our behavior grows more precise with experience.

Young animals are so obviously and endearingly awkward. A young bird, down still sticking out between its growing feathers, hopped up to a bug and swallowed it. A few seconds later, the bird coughed it out. Afterward, the bird kept shaking its head with its tongue stuck out in a genuine "yuck" expression.

Each of us encounters such lessons as we grow up. As we grow, we learn how to refine our clumsiness. Those who don't learn fast enough don't survive. The behavior of mature animals fits better. The hesitations, mistakes, and adjustments necessary to maintain the Fit become more subtle. If I overlook them, I will see generic animals going about their behaviors instead of individuals constantly maintaining their unique Fit. I will simply see deer grazing and not notice individuals actively balancing the need to eat with the need to look around for danger.

⌒

When birds land on a perch, they generally glide in lower than the perch and then swoop upward. This final upward swoop slows the bird so that it can land lightly upon the perch—whether it be a telephone wire, a branch, or a rocky ledge. We can watch and rate these landings the same way a judge watches a gymnast's final dismount. How well does the landing fit with the physical laws of gravity and momentum? How skilled is this individual?

Young birds score 3s and 4s. One young turkey vulture came in too fast for his landing on the branch of a dead Douglas fir. The vulture swooped up to the branch and grabbed it with his talons. His momentum then carried the youth well forward of his balancing point. A second later, the vulture was hanging from the branch upside down. He hung there several seconds as if unsure what to do next. Zero.

Most adults score 8s and 9s (or they would not have survived to adulthood). Usually the bird's speed carries it a few inches above the perch; the bird then lightly drops or flutters down onto the perch. Better to come in a little too high rather than a little too low. Other times, a bird is not centered over its feet when it lands. It must flutter its wings to regain balance.

A kingbird came in for a landing on a swinging telephone wire. Despite strong winds, she swooped up—and was perched with balanced stillness upon a wire swaying wildly back and forth. A perfect 10.

⌒

Watching for the constantly adjusting Fit between an animal and its world has changed the way I see animals. When I first started watching animals, my standard question was "What is the name of that animal?" That question made me rely on external authorities such as identification books and rangers. If I was alone, the question could not be answered. And whenever the question was answered, the answer did not lead to further questions. Thinking I now knew the animal, I would walk away in search of animals with other names. Yet all I really knew were names.

Many years later my standard question has shifted to "What is this animal doing?" This question does not rely on external authorities but turns me back to closer observation of the animal. Searching for the answer leads into other questions, such as "How does this behavior fit?" and "What will this individual do next?" When I recommended these questions to people on my nature walks, our walks settled into extended observations that taught us all. Focusing on names deflects from the moment, whereas watching for the Fit probes the moment. One sees more stories and is inspired more often by pieces of the world fitting together so beautifully.

The maneuvering of a gull flock within a thermal appeared chaotic until I focused on one bird at a time. Then I saw individual birds spiraling upward within the narrow column of rising air. A gliding bird, like a gliding skier, is always descending. But if a gliding bird descends through a strong updraft of warm air that is rising faster than the bird's descent, then the bird will be lifted higher above the ground. Although my focus shifted from one gull to another, my focus kept returning to one particular bird. Its whiteness caught my eye. This gull was remarkably white (which meant it was an older gull). But what held my attention was its lightness and its mastery. The other gulls spiraled relentlessly upward. Yet this bird would actually descend through the spiral to the bottom of the flock, balance in a stall position, and float straight upward through the flock without needing to spiral. It fit perfectly within that thermal. This bird appeared to play, as if waiting for the others to reach the top. It descended again through the ascending flock. Then it floated to the top of the spiraling flock, turned out of the thermal, and glided away on a straight course. As the other birds reached that elevation, they turned and followed.

But of course! It makes sense that a flock should follow a master of updrafts, because such a bird can lead others farther with less effort. Recognizing that bird's mastery would be easy. The gull caught my eye one hundred yards away. It would be even more obvious to the birds in the thermal: Just a few feet from your wingtip, a very white bird drops through the rising flock, then quickly rises straight past you. A master!

Seeing through the Eyes
of Animals

⌒

*T*HE DESERT BIRDS MADE a great fuss. I followed their
scolding sounds to a creosote bush filled with fourteen birds of
five species. They did not fly away as I drew closer. Such a concentration
of birds is unusual in the sparse desert. I looked around for a reason and
there, coiled beneath the bush, lay a rattlesnake.

Another desert afternoon, I saw turkey vultures swooping low over
the desert brush. I went out to investigate and found a deer, freshly killed
by a mountain lion. The blood had not yet clotted.

I have only two eyes, but there are thousands of other eyes around me
seeing the world from different perspectives. The behavior of animals
can lead my eyes to things I would otherwise not see.

⌒

I sat beside a desert waterfall, enjoying its green coolness. Algae and
moss covered much of the slope so that the water slid quietly or dripped
soothingly. A horizontal crack, six inches high, cut across this moist
slope. A canyon wren flew to this crack. It hopped about within the
crack, one eye cocked upward. Every few seconds, the wren jumped with
a flutter of wings and stretched its bill toward the ceiling. This strange
behavior continued for several minutes. What was it doing? After the
wren left, I went over and looked into the crack. Moist moss covered the
dark ceiling. Insects covered the moss.

Now I understood. The small bodies of insects are very susceptible
to dehydration. (That is why many insects emerge in the cool of the

evening.) The shade and moist moss made the ceiling of the crack a perfect refuge from the daytime heat. These conditions attracted a concentration of insects, making the crack an ideal foraging stop for wrens.

I looked around and noticed shadowy cracks everywhere. A trove of juicy insects might be lying within each dark, cool crack. For a few seconds, I saw the desert through a wren's eyes.

⌒

A cormorant is a master at feeding in the heavy winter surf surging between rocks. I could never survive there; the waves and rocks would grind me into fish food. The cormorant, however, swims smoothly within this crashing chaos, diving and feeding. Will the bird dive when this next wave comes? No, the bird moves behind a rock that creates a shelter of calm water. As the wave recedes, the bird flows with it into another tidepool. As I watch the cormorant respond to each wave, what first seemed a chaos of swirling water resolves into complex yet predictable currents shifting with every wave. By moving into these currents with a few strokes of its feet, the cormorant can ride effortlessly to any part of the tidepools. The surging surf connects all the tidepools.

⌒

I sit in a small meadow perched on a mountain ridge a hundred feet below the rocky summit. The tiny alpine tundra plants around me seem so fragile and yet they survive eight months of snow, wind, and sub-freezing temperatures. Being small actually helps them survive. They hunker down out of the wind.

I lie down to examine these plants more closely. After several seconds, I notice a small beetle crawling through the vegetation. As it passes over and under the tangle of stems, it crosses the path of a smaller kind of beetle. "Oh," I think, and switch my attention onto the smaller animal to follow its life for awhile. In a short time, that beetle crosses paths with an even smaller beetle. "Oh," I think, and shift my focus onto the smallest beetle. During its wandering, this beetle encounters several other members of its species. The tundra is full of these minute insects. When they meet, their antennae touch together with enough synchrony to suggest more than a random vibration. What information are they transmitting back and forth?

I move closer so my nose is against the ground. I become completely absorbed into a complex world one inch across. Suddenly, a monstrously large creature appears. Only after several disorienting seconds do I recognize this monster as the small beetle that had first caught my eye.

My tiniest of beetles comes to a round, red thing and passes its feet and feelers over the surface. "What is it? Probably a seed. What kind of plant did it come from?" I look around a bit, half inch this way, half inch that way, until I see a plant with several similar seeds still ripening on it. I smile at the image of this plant as a fruit tree towering an inch above this miniature forest floor. I look closely at the plant and I can see a scar where a seed separated from the plant. The seed would have dropped and come to rest slightly downslope. I look down and there is the seed my beetle is exploring.

So that is where the seed came from. This miniature world makes sense. It is as orderly as mine when it comes to the laws of nature. I follow my beetle farther. It crawls up a stem to the underside of a leaf and starts to lay eggs. I look on the underside of other leaves and see other tiny bubbles of eggs. This inch-wide world is stable enough to allow these insects to find enough food and lay enough eggs to carry on, generation after generation.

The beetles sharpen my focus so that I see details I normally would not see. A square inch fills my attention. Without thinking, I sit up. Suddenly, I am looking at hundreds of square miles of mountains and valleys stretching to the horizon. It's like walking out of a darkened theater into the blinding sunlight. I am staggered. As my mind blinkingly makes the adjustment, I start seeing individual mountains. On their upper flanks, I can see the special green of tundra meadows. "There are miles and miles of this tundra world and each square inch of it is this rich with sense and detail."

Details that I overlook are of critical importance to another species. Animals must have different perspectives on the world because they have different relationships with the world. Their senses must have different sensitivities for exploring different realms. If I watch carefully, any animal can be my teacher, leading me to new places of understanding.

The vultures taught me that this canyon wall faced the autumn sunrise directly. No other part of the canyon warmed up as fast.

For a few weeks before autumn migration, all the local vultures gathered near one of the cliff dwellings where I led tours. Each evening, the vultures roosted in the tall Douglas fir trees at the head of the canyon. Each morning, they glided downcanyon to the cliff dwelling. There, at the base of a massive canyon wall, they began to glide back and forth. No wings flapped. With subtle twists of tails and wings, the silent vultures followed the cliff face across and then turned to cross it again. More vultures glided in from upcanyon, until a hundred vultures were congregated before that sheer canyon wall. So closely did they trace the contours of the cliff face that their shadows slid across the rock just a few inches off their wingtips. These gliding shadows looked like vultures, doubling the apparent size of the swarm. Back and forth, back and forth, the birds and shadows moved. And then, as the morning grew warmer, they began to rise. Faster and faster the silent swarm ascended the cliff until, one by one, each vulture floated over the top and sailed away on a new day's search for something dead.

This spectacular swarm of vultures taught me that this seven hundred-foot wall faced the autumn sunrise directly. No other cliff warmed up as fast. As this cliff warmed, the air touching it warmed and began to rise like a hot air balloon. This rising air provided an early morning seven hundred-foot free elevator ride for the vultures. This free ride was the reason all the vultures flocked to this canyon when the summer heat weakened into the cool mornings of autumn.

I hiked to the top of that cliff one morning so I could look straight down onto the backs of a hundred vultures rising toward me. I felt the sunrise's invisible magic on the air; a warm updraft blew against my face. As the vultures rose by me just a few feet away, I heard them. They made no call. I heard simply the sound of six feet of wing cutting through the air—a gentle but constant breezy swoosh. And now I know that even on the stillest desert afternoon, the soaring vulture hears not the silence but the constant gentle sound of its wings. What does a turn or the strengthening of an updraft sound like? And when the vulture finally does find a carcass and descends for the meal, the swooshing sound accompanies him until he lands. And then, after hours of that constant hum, sudden complete silence, like a silent prayer before dinner.

Edges Dissolve
into Gradients

~c~

ALYSIA AND I SAT on the edge of a woodland meadow. I was pointing out that the sky overhead is deep blue, but the sky near the horizon is whitish blue. Out of the corner of my eye, I can see the edge where the deep blue becomes whitish blue. Yet if I focus on that edge, it disappears. The edge turns into a smooth gradient of darker blue changing imperceptibly into lighter blue. My brain wants to break this gradient of changing color into two regions and concentrate the transition into a sharp edge. But this edge cannot survive direct observation. At no point along this smooth gradient can my eyes say, "The change happens right there."

Apparent edges dissolve under a precise focus; the sky becomes amazingly full of different blues. One gradient of blue stretches from horizon to zenith while another gradient of blue stretches from the Sun to the opposite side of the sky. Slightly darker blue columns of shade slant down from each puffy summer cloud.

Alysia looked around and soon presented me with a ripening acorn. I saw a green acorn with a band of brown at its tip. But when she drew my attention to the edge between the brown and the green, that edge changed into smaller bands of brownish greens and greenish browns. I sharpened my focus onto the edges between these smaller bands. Suddenly, all bands were gone. I saw a gradient of green ripening into brown with the most amazing spectrum of unknown colors within it. A gradient contains the infinite number of gradations by which two regions merge together.

I hiked westward through the Grand Canyon for a week. The trail followed the Tonto Plateau, a gentle, half-mile wide slope about two-thirds of the way down into the canyon. Side canyons cut across the Tonto every five to ten miles. The trail winds down into each side canyon and ascends the other side back onto the plateau. During the heat of midday, I would rest beside desert streams in the peaceful beauty of these side canyons. When the day cooled into late afternoon, I filled my canteens with water and followed the trail back up onto the Tonto. I liked to sleep up on the plateau because it was so vast and still.

Within a few nights, I found that a certain layer of a distinctive brown rock offered a great bedroom. The rock had weathered into a level soil nicely soft for sleeping and the rock layer, or strata, was just high enough above the Tonto to afford panoramic views. Although this strata was less than a foot thick where I first discovered it, its color and position made it easy to find. Each day I browsed another five miles or so westward and each night I hiked up to my bedroom strata.

One night the threat of rain forced me to camp beneath a different rock layer. When I climbed up to my bedroom strata the following night, I found my path blocked by a seven-foot cliff. The cliff was the same distinctive brown and in the same position as my bedroom strata. When I finally found a way to climb to its top, I found the same delightful sleeping facilities. My strata had thickened to seven feet!

Encountering this thickening helped me recall what I had read about the Grand Canyon's geology. This region has risen and subsided many times over hundreds of millions of years. Whenever the land subsided below sea level, a sea moved in from the west and covered the region. When the land rose again, the sea would recede to the west. Therefore, areas farther to the west were beneath the ancient seas longer, and had more time to accumulate sea-floor sediments, which eventually became the layers of rock exposed in the Grand Canyon. This westward gradient of thickening rock binds the length of the canyon into a memory of the land rising above and subsiding beneath the sea almost as if breathing. A thickening of five feet over thirty miles escapes the eye but not the body that has to climb over it.

I sat on an Arctic ridge peacefully gazing down upon a wilderness valley. Ground squirrels and marmots foraged along the ridge or lay sunning on rocks. Somewhere out of sight, far along the ridge, a marmot whistled a shrill alarm. Other marmots whistled and the alarm passed along the ridge like a gust of wind. Animals scurried to their burrows. I looked around; I could see no danger. A golden eagle suddenly appeared close by, gliding fast and low, scanning the slope for any animal that had roamed too far from shelter. Constantly adjusting its large wings to each change in contour, the eagle flew a few feet above the uneven slope with intense, deadly alertness, ready to bank, pursue, and dive in any direction.

The eagle was trying to fly under the warning system of the marmots. An eagle would have a life of fattened ease if it could be invisible, if its only connection with its prey was sharp talons sinking into flesh. But a gradient of alarm lay between the eagle and the marmots. The marmots tried to extend the gradient by warning each other and the eagle tried to narrow the gradient by flying low, but neither could escape the gradient that will connect them throughout their lives.

We live within gradients. A gradient of thinning atmosphere intervenes between my lungs and the vacuum of outer space. Just as a gradient of vibrations along the web can guide the spider to the struggling fly, so a gradient of increasingly wider, busier roads can guide me from my driveway to the nearest highway. Just as the marmots' gradient of alarm alerted me to the unseen eagle, so other gradients can bring me news of unseen things. I sense that I am approaching a stream through gradients of smells, bird songs, and larger leaves. I sense that I am approaching a city through gradients of increasing traffic, billboards, radio stations, and night glow in the sky. Noticing gradients connects me more richly with this world.

Nevertheless, something inside me tends to concentrate these gradients into edges that break the world into many independent objects. This is an acorn; over there is a rock. I notice the edges between things rather than the interconnections within and between them. This preference makes sense. Gentle gradients pose no immediate threat but we must recognize the edges of danger. We must be able to spot the camouflaged outline of a predator stalking slowly through the vegetation. Therefore the eyes and brain have evolved a sensitivity to edges. A world of visually separated objects is the kind of world I usually practice thinking about.

But when I practice focusing precisely on edges, a world of separating edges becomes a world of interconnecting gradients. Gradients merge realms I once thought of as distinct. Where is the edge between land and sea? Perhaps the edge is where the waves meet the land. But where is that meeting place? Is it offshore where the bottom of the wave's energy contacts the land and the wave begins to rise into a breaker? Or is it where the wave breaks? Or is it the highest point wetted by the wave? No matter where I draw the line, it shifts with every wave, tide, and season.

Perhaps the edge is out beyond the sight of land or farther out beyond the sight of land birds. Or maybe the edge lies in the other direction. Large logs lie high and dry far up on the beach. Winter storm waves shoved them there. Do they mark the edge? Or is it the wispy edges of the coastal fog several miles inland?

A university professor installed a seismograph at the park in Texas where I worked. One day, the seismograph printed out a series of rhythmic pulses, hour after hour. Something was causing the bedrock to vibrate—though only a sensitive machine could detect it. The professor called to tell us that the vibrations were being caused by massive storm waves smashing against the Alaskan coast. Where is the edge between land and sea?

The Gradient of
Converging Water

⟋⟍

W HEN I WAS SIXTEEN, I prepared for my first solo
hike. My simple map showed only lakes, streams, trails,
and major mountain peaks. I studied the map, planning possible routes
and fantasizing about all the places I would explore. Part of the map
showed two rivers flowing parallel to one another, each with a trail beside
it. Between these two trails were several mountain peaks. I planned to
leave one trail and walk through the gap between peaks to the other trail.

When I arrived at the trailhead, I found that the two rivers (with their
trails) flowed along the bottoms of two deep glacial valleys. The valleys

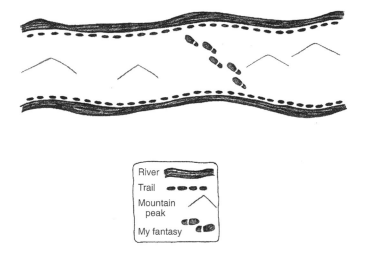

Imagination runs wild when there is no connection between mountains and rivers.

were separated by a three thousand-foot-high, continuous mountain ridge whose highest points were the mountain peaks marked on my map. No way was I going to stroll across from one trail to the other.

That memory reminds me of how I once saw the world. Summits and rivers existed completely independently of one another, with no influence whatsoever on the land in between them. In a world as disconnected as that, I had to stick to the trails if I wanted to find my way. Yet I did learn some things that day. I learned that a summit is surrounded by a mountain and that a river is surrounded by a valley. I began to learn about the drainage patterns that water has carved upon all the land.

These drainage patterns were unknown to me as a child because I grew up in a town. Every town is built upon a pattern of streams but most towns have encased their streams in culverts and buried them beneath pavement. Raindrops begin to converge into streams, but then they disappear through grates down into the storm sewers. Streams are allowed to flow freely only through parks, so I encountered streams as disjointed scenery that appeared at one end of a park and disappeared at the other end. The intricate, subtle slopes of a drainage have been graded and covered with smooth sidewalks and roads. We become what we practice, so in towns we learn the pattern of streets rather than the pattern of drainages. Not until I felt the subtle slopes underfoot as I hiked across deserts and mountains did I learn the pattern of drainages.

⌒

I came to this kind of hiking with a road map mentality; the shortest distance between two points is a straight line. But a straight line across the land will keep rising and falling. I puffed up one slope and then dropped down the other side, only to puff up another slope. This constant change in breathing tired me out. The land felt like a series of obstacles.

After enough of this clambering, the land started to shape my path of shortest distance into the path of least resistance. Now, I try to flow around ridges rather than straight over them. My straight line begins to melt into graceful curves that contour the land. My always-changing breathing calms into a steady, sustained breathing as powerful as the steady yet gentle ascension of the always curving path.

As I curve back and forth, I start to notice patterns. I might notice, for example, that every time I start to curve to the left, the view starts to open up. The plants grow further apart and the view through them extends further. But when I start to curve to the right, the land curves in to embrace me. Plants grow more abundantly. My view closes in. I find myself in a more intimate setting of flowers and bird songs. Then the path begins its curve to the left and the world opens once again. Like my steady breathing, the land alternately opens and contracts.

These patterns transform my awareness: A path curving back and forth becomes a path curving in and out of drainages. I curve into and through a drainage and out and around the ridge that divides drainages. Within each drainage, the curves of the land gather soil moisture from the surrounding slopes. The plants, insects, and birds respond to this greater abundance with greater abundance. But out of the ridges, there are no moisture-providing slopes above. Soil moisture and the life it supports is less. The view opens.

On the ridges, the slopes are below. In the drainages, the slopes rise above. Along each curve of my path, the slopes rise and subside around me. With every curve a gradient of soil moisture rises and subsides, expressing itself uniquely with every different facing of slope, with changing elevation. The path pulses with soil moisture. Feet feel it in the ground.

The curving path is not a simple repetition of in and out. Every step is simultaneously in and out different scales within a complex network of drainages. I can be walking into one drainage at the same time I am walking out of a larger drainage and yet deeper into an even larger drainage. Because of this nesting, the experience of the land curving in to embrace me with a drainage is different every time.

If I'm walking across dry land, for example, I am usually crossing the slight, gentle curves of micro-drainages, wet only during a heavy rain. Sometimes the only hint is the slight curve in the trail that draws my attention to the plants growing a little higher, a little closer together. The rhythm of these micro-drainages are punctuated every now and then by a larger drainage with an occasional tree lining its route. And after an hour of these ins and outs, I come to the center of the mother drainage, a rocky cascade, green shade beneath overarching trees.

So too, with the ridges. Most are so subtle I don't perceive them as divides, only as bends in the trail. Others push me far enough out to make me look around. And every hour or so, I walk out around a divide . . . and a whole new landscape swings into view. I stop for a snack break and to gaze for an hour.

Drainages nest so I can be hiking into one *drainage at the same time I am hiking* out *of a larger drainage at the same time I am hiking* into *an even larger drainage.*

But it is not that regular. Every piece of land has a different rhythm depending on its moistness, the nature of its bedrock, the steepness of its slopes, and where I am within even greater drainages. In some regions, the streams are five minutes apart; in others, they are only springs several hours apart. In some regions, I see only a hundred feet through the forest; in others, I gaze perpetually out over tens of miles to distant mountain ranges.

All the land is a complex nesting of drainages. I feel its sensual shape with every step when my path fits the land.

⌒

The fundamental pattern is convergence. Water joins together as it flows downhill. A myriad streams concentrate to a "focus" in a large river. This pattern of convergence is as true on a small scale at the head of a drainage as it is on a large scale. The pattern of convergence creates a gradient of increasing size and volume along the length of a stream.

This gradient of increasing volume creates an accompanying gradient of increasing speed. I can see this gradient of increasing speed on a rain-splattered window. The upper part of the window is dotted with individual raindrops. These individual raindrops remain stationary because even smooth, vertical glass has enough friction to resist gravity's pull on small raindrops. But when two raindrops join, their combined weight overcomes this frictional resistance. The combined droplet begins to creep down the window and runs into other stationary drops, which join it. As the droplet grows, it flows faster until it runs into one of the rivulets streaming off the window. Gradients of increasing size and speed extend from individual raindrops at the window top to rivulets at the bottom.

Converging water flows faster. This pattern is as true of streams as it is for raindrops. Two separate streambeds contain more frictional resistance than a single, combined streambed (see the illustration on the following page for an explanation). Less friction allows the larger, combined stream to flow faster.

These gradients of increasing volume and increasing speed interact to create a third gradient of increasing force. As a trillion raindrops converge into a thousand tiny rivulets that converge into a stream, the force of the growing, accelerating mass increases.

I experienced the increasing force of converging water when I rafted down an Oregon river in late May, a time when rivers are swollen by snowmelt from the mountains. The river flowed steep, full, and fast. Chuting between boulders and cresting standing waves, I experienced exuberant rushes of adrenaline. Each day, I floated more than twenty miles.

On the fourth day, the river converged with the snowmelt-swollen Snake River, a large river of the Northwest. I found myself on a very different river. There were no rapids or waves. But upwellings rose to the surface, noisily pushed the current apart for many seconds, and then faded away. Swirls of energy formed whirlpools four feet across that pulled the surface of the river down several inches. I rode on the surface of an enormous mass of water flowing very fast. The river carried me more than twenty miles in a few hours.

I felt apprehensive the entire time; the smooth quietness of the Snake's power was spooky. The current was so powerful that when my raft swept into one of its eddies, I could not get out. I tried to paddle out,

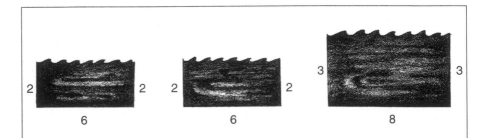

On the left are cross-sections of two small streams; on the right is the cross-section of the larger stream formed by their convergence. This larger stream holds the same amount of water as the two small streams. (Each small stream has a cross-sectional area of 2 x 6 = 12 square feet. Together the two small streams hold 24 square feet. The large stream has a cross-sectional area of 3 x 8 = 24 square feet.) The volume of water does not change when the streams converge. What does change is the area of streambed surface the water must flow across. Each small stream has 2 + 6 + 2 = 10 feet, so the two streams together have 20 feet of streambed surface. The large stream, however, has only 3 + 8 + 3 = 14 feet of surface. The same volume of flowing water encounters less surface, and therefore less friction, in the single, larger stream, allowing the water to flow faster after it converges. Flowing faster reduces the depth, which reduces the surface area even more.

but surges of water from the main current kept pushing me back into the eddy. I circled there for an hour, watching giant logs in the main current rush past me like logging trucks.

Everything about that huge, smooth, quiet river was on a different scale than the smaller, splashier, fun river. On the small river, I was aware of swirling water slowed by a rough streambed of boulders a few feet below the surface. I could hear those boulders being clunked and chipped by rocks. On the Snake River, the water flowed deep, unencumbered, smooth, and fast. I could neither see nor hear the bottom, though I could imagine boulders down there tumbling to the sea.

⌐

As water converges, it gathers the power to erode its path into the land. The path is etched lightly in the headwaters, where water has little power, and is gouged more deeply downstream as the water gathers its power. Converging drainage patterns have given their shape to the land. The gradients of converging water connect the mountains to the sea. These gradients can guide me through unknown country. I can wander without a map through country without a trail. I navigate by slope, streambed, and drainage divide rather than by north, south, east, and west. Though my route twists and turns, I stay oriented by whether the land, when it curves to the left, leads me toward a drainage or a divide. Wherever I roam—desert, tundra, or mountains—flowing water has already made its path.

The Edge of Balance

⌒

*T*HE ONLY SOUND WITHIN the narrow, desert canyon was the soothing sound of a small waterfall at the outlet of a pool. In the pool, a water skipper drifted with the current. The current quickened as it neared the waterfall but the insect, standing upon the water's surface tension, drifted on. Would it be carried over the waterfall? The current was accelerating dramatically. Just as I became sure the water skipper would be swept away, it skipped back up into the pool, stopped, and again drifted slowly toward the waterfall. Again and again, just as I thought the accelerating current would sweep it away, the water skipper skipped away from the waterfall.

Drifting down a gradient toward an edge.

The drifting water skipper focused my attention on the smooth changes within the current. As the stream constricted from the deep pool to the narrow lip of the waterfall, the current accelerated from a broad, slow flow to a chute of plunging water. This acceleration was as smooth as the stream-molding bedrock.

For the water skipper, however, there was a point along that smooth gradient of accelerating water where the current became too strong. That point formed an edge beyond which the water skipper would not drift. It drifted toward that edge but then skipped back up, drifted down, skipped back up. . . .

⌒⌒

Even though a gradient is gentle and smooth, there can be a point along it where some relationship shifts. This shift is like walking up a teeter-totter. I can move toward the center and the teeter-totter remains in the same position. Yet when I cross a certain point, maybe only an inch away from where I stood before, the balance shifts and the teeter-totter tips in the other direction.

That crouching fox waited for the squirrel to move far enough along the gradient of decreasing distance to shift the advantage from the squirrel to the fox. At the rock-throwing overlook, my reluctance to turn back increased as I walked farther away until the balance shifted. That point was marked by the edge between no rocks left on the ground and rocks still lying on the ground.

Noticing edges often leads me to see the underlying gradients they Fit with. The colorful edge between two species of wildflowers led me to notice a gradient of clay soil turning into sandy soil. Noticing this gradient then helps me understand the edge. Edges cease being boundaries that separate; they mark a shifting balance within the gradients that connect.

⌒⌒

When I began hiking, I was often frustrated by a seemingly perverse characteristic of trails. Whenever a broad, smooth, level trail starts up a steep slope, it inevitably turns into a narrow trough, tangled with tree roots and spiked with bedrock. A steep trail is hard enough; the precarious footing of the tangled trough adds insult to injury. Why can't the steep trails be broad and smooth and let the level parts be messy? Only after I grew familiar with the ways of water did I understand this pattern.

Trails are also paths for water. When rainwater and melted snow flow down a steep trail, the flow accelerates and acquires the energy to erode. Erosion deepens a steep trail into a gully. The only things left behind in the trail are the roots and bedrock that can't be washed away. But as the trail levels out at the bottom of the hill, the water slows down, loses the energy to erode, and drops the soil it carries. The deposited soil forms a broad, smooth surface for the trail. Erosion shifts to deposition and a narrow trough shifts to a broad, flat trail.

This shifting point between erosion and deposition gives a special shape to cinder cones. A cinder cone forms where a volcanic vent spatters lava into the air. The lava falls as cinders around the erupting vent. A pile accumulates. If the slope of this pile is gentle, then the cinders falling on it will remain there and build up the slope, making it steeper. But when the slope becomes too steep, the falling cinders begin to tumble down the slope. The slope can't grow any steeper than this. Geologists call this degree of steepness (about 30°) the angle of repose. It marks the steepest slope at which the accumulating cinders won't tumble or slump.

I sat near the top of a nine hundred-foot-high cinder cone wondering what would happen to a rock that I tried rolling down this special slope. Would it not roll or what? I gently pushed a cinder. It rolled down the slope. It did not speed up or slow down. It was not stopped by any rock nor did it dislodge any other rock. My slight push had made that particular rock unstable on this slope. It just kept rolling slowly but relentlessly down the quarter-mile-long slope until it reached the bottom, where it promptly stopped.

If the slope had been any gentler, the rock would have slowed down and stopped upon the slope. If the slope had been any steeper, the rock would have picked up speed until it had enough energy to dislodge other rocks. But the slope lay poised between these two possibilities.

⌣

After leaking helium for several days, my daughter's balloon no longer bobbed against the ceiling. It drifted at half mast, its string dangling onto the floor. When I pushed the balloon up toward the ceiling, it rose, pulling the string off the floor. But the balloon did not have enough lift to carry the weight of the entire string. The balloon stopped rising and began to sink. The balloon settled with increasing speed until the string contacted the floor. As more of the string settled onto the floor, the balloon's load grew lighter. The balloon's descent slowed and then stopped. Now the balloon, freed of most of the string's weight, had enough lift to rise again. But as it rose, it lifted the string with it. The higher the balloon ascended, the heavier its load of string grew. Eventually the balloon was again too heavy and it settled down toward the floor once again. Moving higher increased the load; moving lower decreased the load. The balloon oscillated up and down, eventually coming to rest at the point where the balloon's load balanced with its lift.

⌒

Edges come lightly to balance on the shifting point along a gradient. There is a beauty in the oscillating Fit between edge and gradient. Edges are not rigid, stiff, or fixed. They have a shimmering, vibrating quality, a potential for moving back and forth almost as if the edges were breathing.

In some places, the Arctic timberline lies balanced on a gradient of permafrost. Above timberline, the permafrost lies too close to the surface to allow trees to grow. Below timberline, the ground thaws deeply enough each summer to allow trees to grow. Right at timberline, the soil thaws deeply enough to allow a spruce seed to sprout. A tree grows. Yet as it grows, it shades the ground beneath it. The shaded, cooler ground no longer thaws deeply enough each summer. The tree dies, loses its needles, and falls over. Now sunlight can reach the ground and warm it again. The permafrost thaws deeply enough for another seed to sprout. That tree and its shadow grow. . . .

Change shifts edges. If a long-term warming trend occurs in the Arctic, timberline creeps higher. If streamflow diminishes, the water skipper can drift closer to the waterfall. If the fox is weary, the squirrel must move closer before the advantage shifts to the fox.

A shifting edge alerts me to change. I glanced at the sloping rock edge of a small pond as I walked across a mountain meadow one morning. The edge between water and dry rock caught my eye because it was a rising edge. I looked up. The snowbanks on the slope above were facing the early morning sun. The snow was melting up there, making the ponds and streams rise down here. I marked the water's edge with pebbles. By midday, they were underwater.

Marking edges helps me grow more aware of change. I mark the edge of a melting snowbank with pine cones and am amazed to find the entire snowbank gone by evening. I mark with sticks how far waves advance up the beach to check whether the tide is coming in or going out. I mark the edge of a clump of plants with stones to find out if the plants are expanding their range. Each year I mark the edge of spring by celebrating the first bird songs I hear.

The Tracks of Change

⌒

*T*HE CHIPMUNK BIT OFF the dandelion's unopened seed head and carried it to the top of a log where he could look out for danger. The chipmunk quickly ate the bottom of the seed head, dropped the top of it on the log, and scurried off to harvest another.

What a perfect way to eat dandelion seeds! Within days, these seed heads will open into white bubbles of fluff to be scattered by the wind. If chipmunk tried to harvest the seeds then, most of the seeds would drift away. Fluff would tickle its nostrils and coat its mouth. Harvesting seeds then would be absurd. But today, a hundred ripe seeds are concentrated at the bottom of each seed head. A chipmunk can eat them all and not have to contend with the fluff developing at the upper end of the seed head.

The chipmunk ate several seed heads. The discarded tops formed a pile of matted fluff that marked this chipmunk's lunch spot. Once I understood how these piles formed, I began to notice them on logs throughout the forest.

⌒

A rock broke from the cliff and bounded down the snowfield. Snow sprayed out from each crunching impact, creating white scars of freshly exposed snow. As the rock slowed, its bounces became shorter, until the rock rolled to a stop.

Other dark rocks lay on the snow. Upslope of each lay a similar trail of white scars. Each trail could be traced back up the snowbank to a fresh scar on the cliff where its rock had broken.

Many changes pass quickly but the ending state of that change (such as the pile of discarded seed heads) remains for some time. Therefore, ending states are easier to see than the changes themselves. They are like tracks. The tracks of a wolf are easier to see than the wolf itself. By noticing the tracks of change, I become more aware of changes that happen constantly but are rarely seen.

⌒

The dipper (a bird found only near fast-moving freshwater streams) flew to a rock standing in mid-stream. The dipper squatted and defecated a white splotch onto the rock. The moment I saw that splotch form, I began to notice other white splotches on other rocks in the stream. I had hiked this way four days ago and never noticed those splotches. I notice some details only when something such as the squat of a dipper tells their story. A large section of the unknown lies visible before my eyes but invisible to my mind.

As I searched for dipper droppings, I began to notice older, more faded droppings. Rock surfaces had subtle mosaics of white, gray, and brown droppings. A gradient of color revealed older droppings beneath fresher droppings. The drier boulders accumulated the richest mosaics. This drew my attention to how the stream splashed, washed, and cleaned rocks differently depending on their size and position within the stream. As I looked at the size and location of each boulder, I realized that each rock is a track of change. Each rock has a story of how it came to be where it is. The same could be said about the stream, the trees growing beside it, the mountains, the clouds, the atmosphere: None of these existed at the beginning of time. Each one is a track of change that helps tell the story of how the world came to be what it is at this moment.

Tracks of change cover the world with stories. When I look closely at shale, I see fine, orderly layers of sediment made from silt that settled to the bottom of ancient seas. Large floods, however, could carry larger grains of silt into the sea. These larger grains formed a microscopically thin layer of slightly sandier shale. Two hundred million years later, the rock now breaks along this layer. It is as if the silt grains said to each other, "I am not of you. Even though we all came to this place two hundred million years ago, you came a month later after the flood. I am not of you—even after being bound together for two hundred million years. This is our falling apart and we shall now go our separate ways."

Grains of beach sand are different colors. Two grains lying beside each other might have originated from the rock of mountain ranges hundreds of miles apart. Each grain of sand is a track of change, yet all these tracks blend into a smooth beach upon which the waves and walkers take turns leaving fresher tracks.

Seeing Further into the
Fourth Dimension

⟳

NOT UNTIL EVENING, when all the buttercups were staring me right in the face, did I finally understand what was happening. All day we had been hiking east across the Arctic tundra. Everywhere, newly-arrived birds sang as they hurried to start nesting. A week ago, patches of snow mottled a brown tundra, but the long days of early June transform this land with astonishing speed. The tundra was now green despite the cool days and still frosty short nights. White buttercups, the first flowers of the tundra spring, bloomed everywhere

By evening, we were hiking up a gentle slope toward a mountain pass. The low Sun behind us illuminated a spectacular display of buttercups. White petals glowing golden in the Sun's evening light covered the slope. We walked for many minutes in mindless appreciation until I began to wonder why the buttercups were so spectacularly abundant on this particular slope.

I turned to look back on all the buttercups we had just walked past. There weren't any. The tundra stretched green without a single white flower. I turned back upslope and there glowed millions of buttercups. I looked back and forth in confusion. Millions of buttercups grew ahead of me, none behind me. As I looked to either side, I realized I was surrounded by millions of flowers all facing one direction.

Then I remembered: Buttercups are heliotropes. Their flowers turn through the day so they always face the sun. When the morning Sun was in the east, all the flowers faced east. Since I had been walking east, I saw mostly the unspectacular green backs of the flowers. In the midday, all the flowers faced south, so I saw the flowers ahead of me from the side. Only in the evening did they stare me right in my eastward-looking face.

I had walked all day in the midst of a billion buttercups without noticing that they were precisely tracking the Sun. If all this turning had happened in just one minute, I would have stared dumbfounded as mile after mile of flowers turned on their stems in eerie synchrony. The reality is just as eerie, but it happens at a rate too slow to notice. If the entire tundra can turn its face as I walk by, what other slow changes do I overlook?

⌇

Snowbanks remain in the summer meadows of high mountains. A continuous blanket of snow covered these meadows throughout the winter but as the snow melted, it thinned into countless separate snowbanks. Each day, the edges of the melting snowbanks recede, exposing more of last year's dead vegetation flattened by nine months of snow. A brown ring of freshly exposed soggy ground surrounds each shrinking snowbank. This brown ring is the track of last week's larger snowbank.

Beyond the brown ring grows green meadow. When I examine the edge between brown ring and green meadow, I discover a gradient of ground drying out and new growth pushing up through the dead vegetation. A few days ago, this greening ground had been the soggy brown ring bordering the snowbank. But in the sunny days since then, the melting snowbank has receded several feet, while the exposed ground has warmed enough for plants to grow.

The farther an area is from the receding snowbank, the longer it has been snow-free and the more growing days its plants have had. These alpine plants must develop quickly, because they have only a few months of growing time before the snow returns. The receding snowbank creates a gradient of plant growth extending out from it.

Near the snowbank, green tips bulge out of the ground. A few feet farther, the tips have grown into leaves. Even farther from the snowbanks, stalks rise above the leaves. Plants still farther away have buds forming on their stalk. Far from the snowbanks, bees buzz around plants in full flower. Farther still, the flowers disappear as the petals drop off and the base of each former flower swells with developing seeds.

By moving across the meadow, I can observe in minute detail a flowering process that requires many days. Moving away from the snowbank is like moving through time.

An oak leaf fluttered down onto a stream. It floated toward me until it lodged against a dam of sodden leaves. The downstream end of the dam was a brownish slimy muck. I examined the edge between freshly fallen leaf and slimy muck and discovered a gradient of decay. By moving downstream from the newly trapped leaf, I could see the entire process of leaf decay within a few inches. Brown spots appeared and expanded until all of a leaf was brown. As the spots expanded, their weakening centers fell apart, revealing the more resistant network of veins within

1

As I move my focus away from the melting snowbank, I see through time.

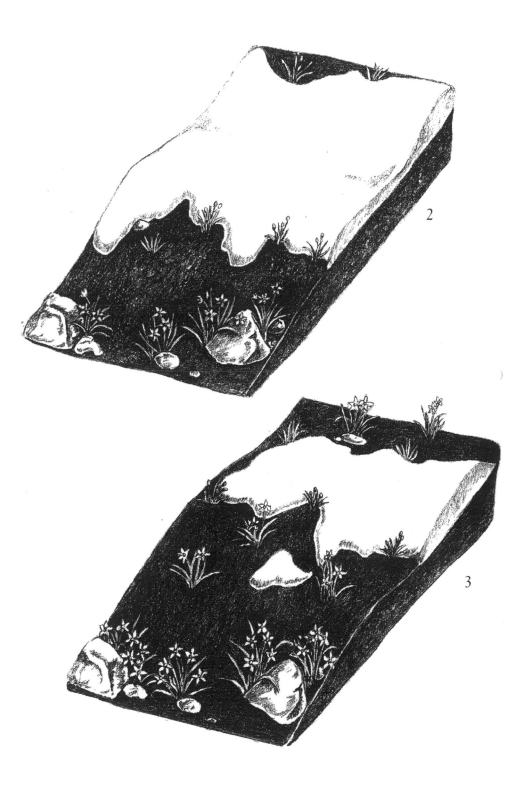

2

3

the leaf. These holes grew larger and more numerous until only the stems and largest veins remained within the brown muck at the downstream end of the dam. Someday the newly fallen fresh leaf would look like that.

⌒

One sunny day, I took a break from writing this book to sit in a meadow. A game came to mind. I pretended I was someone who had just taken a break from reading my book. What might I discover if I tried practicing some of these ideas?

I looked around me. Bees were buzzing. What would I notice if I looked through the eyes of a bee? I focused on the closest bee. It was landing on only one species of plant, which had a spike of many flowers. The bee visited many plants, but always landed only on a central portion of each spike of flowers and never crawled over the entire spike. Something only within that portion of the spike attracted the bee. I sharpened my focus on this area and saw a small ring of flowers in full bloom. Below that ring of blooming flowers were wilted flowers losing their petals. Above that ring of blooming flowers were buds just about to blossom.

This gradient reveals that this plant's flowering starts at the base of the spike and gradually moves upward. By studying the spike from its top to its bottom, I could study the process of flowering from the emergence of the bud through the blossoming stage to the swelling of the seed.

There is wisdom in spreading one's flowering over many days. If a cold storm sweeps in and grounds the pollinating insects for a week, all is not lost. After the storm, flowers coming into bloom higher on the spike will provide another opportunity for pollination. In addition, a plant flowering over a longer time will come in contact with a greater diversity of pollen and will produce a greater genetic diversity of seeds. This increases the chances that a few seeds will grow into the next generation.

⌒

The fallen trees in a forest reveal different stages in the process of tree decay. When I view them in sequence, I can study a process taking many years. The branches of a newly fallen tree hold the trunk off the ground. The trunk remains dry and strong. But ground rot weakens the branches and the trunk settles onto the ground. The soil's moist power of decay enters and softens the trunk. The trunk slowly squishes down-

What would I notice if I looked through the eyes of a bee?

ward, bulging at the sides until it falls apart. The last stage is a fading line of rotting wood chips, a mere shadow of the tree that once lay there. Usually this shadow is lined with saplings. The elements from a former tree rise again above the forest floor.

⌣

A change cannot be run backward. But I can move back and forth through "time." I can look downstream and see leaves rot into a brown slime or move my gaze upstream and watch brown slime freshen into leaves. If I discover some new flowering feature as I move away from the snowbank, I can move back toward the snowbank (back in "time") to study its origin. Moving back and forth helps me sense how things once were and how things will be in the future.

A rock outcrop is inevitably surrounded by rock fragments that have broken off. Recently fallen slabs remain solid while older ones have broken into puzzles of rock fragments. Easy puzzles are found at the base of the outcrop. These recently fragmented rocks are easily reassembled because their pieces lie close together and they fit snugly back together. Older puzzles have crept farther downslope. They are harder to reassemble because their pieces have moved apart, become rounded off, and have broken into even smaller pieces.

Like running a film backward, I can move my eyes over these rocks in a direction that moves back in time. Smaller rocks move upslope, reassembling into slabs that jump up and reattach themselves to the outcrop. The accumulating weight of the returning slabs compresses them back into solid bedrock.

Or I can move forward in time. Cracks penetrate the bedrock, splitting off large slabs and exposing fresh surfaces to be cracked and weathered. Large slabs of rocks are cracked into smaller chunks that move more easily down the slope. As the rocks creep downslope, they weather into smaller pieces, which will crumble into still smaller pieces that are washed into the nearest stream. Eventually, this outcrop will flow as sand to the sea.

Back and forth my eyes move through time, fracturing the rock and sending it down to the sea, calling it back and burying it again. I can move my eyes through space and see further into time.

Spirals of Change

⌒

*T*HE SCHOOL'S EUCALYPTUS TREE was covered with blossoms at different stages of flowering. The students noticed that the early stages had pistil stalks sticking up while the later stages had none. We searched for blossoms in between these two stages and found several. They revealed that the pistils were withering and turning from green to brown. Then the stalks disappeared. They must be falling off. We searched the ground. A girl finally found one. Seeing what the withered stalks looked like made it easy for us to find more and more and more, until we realized we were standing on an overlooked carpet of withered, fallen stalks.

Searching for intermediate stages of a process is a game. Finding in-between stages reveals the smoothness of a process. Tracing this smooth change generates a momentum that leads me to notice more details and discover still more stages. For example, a fresh cow pie lying beside an old dry one got me studying the process by which cow pies break down. The beginning of this process, the deposition of a fresh cow pie, was familiar to me; I had seen it happen many times. When I searched for increasingly older stages of the process, I found cow pies sprouting grass and even older cow pies crumbling within mounds of tall, well-fertilized grass. A spongy mass of roots filled these crumbling cow pies. The oldest cow pies of all were no longer manure; they were patches of lush grass growing in clumps about the diameter of a cow pie. The breakdown of the cow pie nourished the grass whose expanding roots helped break the cow pie apart.

⌒

I can observe how a crack grows by studying cracks within a rock outcrop in order from thinnest to widest. Like a foot in the door, wind-blown dust drops into these cracks and prevents them from closing. A dusty crack retains more moisture than a bare crack, so when the moisture freezes in winter, the dusty crack will be pried a bit more by ice crystals. As the rock is pried apart, dust particles drop deeper into the crack, making space for more wind-blown dust. More dust holds more moisture, which wedges the rock still farther apart, which allows more dust to settle in. Bold plants colonize this dust and send their root hairs prying into the microscopic forerunners of cracks.

This process involves a back and forth spiraling between cause and effect. The dust causes the crack to open more, which causes dust to settle deeper into the crack. Does the accumulated dust cause the crack or does the crack cause the accumulated dust? Both, in a spiral of tiny changes.

I encounter the same back and forth logic in the mountains. Because water flows downhill, the tops of mountains can have only the beginning of streams. As the streams flow down from the summit, they converge with other streams and grow larger. Therefore, the streams must be smallest where the mountains are tallest.

However, the smaller the stream, the less erosive power it possesses. Areas having smaller streams will be eroded less. Therefore the land will be tallest where the streams are smallest. Do the tall mountains cause the small streams or do the small streams cause the tall mountains?

~

The tundra buttercups turning with the Sun are part of another spiral. Their white petals form a parabolic dish, which reflects the sunlight and concentrates its heat near the center of the flower, where the reproductive parts are located. By always facing the Sun, this part stays warm throughout the day, allowing the seeds to develop despite the cool air of early June.

But the flowers must be pollinated by insects before their seeds can develop. Insects cannot create their own heat, so they are sluggish in cold air. Yet like a warm, friendly inn on a cold night, the center of each Sun-following buttercup provides a warm place filled with food. An insect can gather enough energy at one flower to survive the cold flight to the next, nearby flower. The flowers make it possible for insects to be active during this cold season. On the other hand, the insects make it possible for the plants to flower and be pollinated this early. Which caused which? Did the insects make the flowers possible or did the flowers make the insects possible?

They probably made each other possible. The flowers allowed the insects to emerge a bit earlier, which allowed the buttercups to emerge a bit earlier, which allowed the insects to emerge a bit earlier still. Together, over generations, they helped each other rise earlier and earlier into the cold air. Neither is The Cause. The cause lies in their spiraling relationship.

Just as an edge dissolves into a gradient when I focus on it, so cause and effect dissolve into a spiral when I study them. I find myself growing dubious of simple cause and effect statements. If I am told "A causes B", I start wondering how B might also cause A. My notion of cause and effect is often a crude lumping together of a smoother, more subtle process. When I think of change in terms of a simple cause with an effect, I tend to think that large effects require large causes. But when I see cause and effect as a spiral, I understand that large effects can be produced by a very small spiral looping over and over again. Spirals lead me to look smaller. As I open my mind to the significance of smaller changes, I find more and more spirals. They are so abundant that spirals of change have been given many names: vicious cycles, positive feedback loops, reinforcing feedback loops, downward spirals, and co-evolution. The world is full of spirals containing unknown power.

Walking

⌒

*L*EARNING IS THE SPIRAL OF CHANGE I am most familiar with. Each tiny lesson changes thoughts and behaviors. Changed behaviors lead to new experiences which lead to new tiny lessons. Accumulating lessons refine dim awareness into conscious mastery.

An example of such a spiral is learning how to walk. When I first began hiking, I had to stare down at the uneven ground in order to place my feet where I would not trip or stumble. But when I looked at my feet, I could see only a small area. The world at my feet streamed too fast through that small spotlight of attention. I saw obstacles only at the last moment. This narrow focus made me feel a little frantic. Preoccupation with my feet prevented me from growing aware of the world around me.

Yet as I practiced walking, my feet began to learn to take care of themselves. I didn't need to supervise them as closely. My gaze could drift a step ahead. This small shift made such a difference, because now I could see a larger area. The ground within this broader view did not stream underfoot so fast. I had more time to choose where I would step. A spiral of learning between my feet and eyes had begun. As my feet learned to walk on uneven ground with less supervision, my eyes practiced focusing farther ahead, which allowed my feet the practice of walking with even less supervision.

⌒

As a beginning hiker, I had to carry a flashlight when I went walking at night. I pointed the beam of light down around my feet and stared into its bright pool. My eyes adjusted to this brightness, so that when I glanced away, the unlit night appeared dark and impenetrable—which confirmed my need for a flashlight. I became fixated like a moth on light. But a spiral of learning freed my feet to walk without a flashlight. In the darkness, my eyes dilated wide open and saw the mysterious, alluring world of night.

The night world looks different because I see it with different parts of my eyes and brain. Colors dominate my daytime sight, but the color-sensitive part of the eye requires abundant light; it cannot operate in night's dim light. I see the night's light with a part of my eye more sensitive to shapes and bulks. The land takes on an almost palpable weight at night, almost as if my eyes feel the world more than see it.

Dusky owls fly silently low over the ground, back and forth in long hunting swaths. Twice owls have come upon this unilluminated human staring right at them and have swerved away in surprise and then circled several times, observing me.

Night is a quieter world, quiet enough to hear the scurrying of a mouse. In the desert moonlight, a mouse went about its business, staying under overhangs and in the shadows as much as possible. The mouse dashed across the moonlight only when there was no other way to reach another shadow. The mouse never paused in the light. As the moon moves through the night, the shadows will move and the mouse will have to change its path. Perhaps by staying within the shifting shadows, the mouse can forage over most of the ground in the course of the night.

Walking at night opens new areas of learning. Once, I went to a beach to watch the grunion mate. Grunion are small fish that wriggle out of the surf during the night's high tide to mate and lay their eggs in the beach. Other people had flashlights with which they watched individual fish. Not having a flashlight, I walked to a deserted, dark section of the beach. In the calm between the crashing of invisible breakers, I heard the grunion slithering and wriggling. The grunion flashed with a ghostly pale luminescence. I don't know whether the luminescence was caused by the grunion disturbing phosphorescence in the water or if the grunions themselves have luminescence, perhaps so the females can attract the males. This luminescence was as invisible in a flashlight beam as the stars are invisible in the sunlight.

Walking in the night (slowly at first) gives additional practice in walking without watching my feet. I learn to scan farther ahead as I walk, day or night. I begin to notice squirrels dashing up trees and birds dropping into bushes at my approach. I hear their warning calls and chirps. Like a boat moving across a still lake, my movement creates waves of disturbance spreading outward. To see the undisturbed original stillness, I must look out beyond the waves of my disturbance.

I look farther ahead as I walk, and I begin to notice the movements of animals turning their eyes upon me and freezing. If I stop, an animal usually will not run away. By looking farther ahead, I disturb less and see more. I walk within a world more full of life. This abundance of life encourages me to scan still farther ahead.

While walking through the desert one day, I happened to look to the side. What I saw startled me. Objects appeared to move at different speeds depending on their distances from me. Nearby plants streamed though my visual field quickly while more distant plants moved more slowly. As I practiced, I noticed that the near side of a bush appears to move past faster than the far side. Everything takes on a greater sense of depth. Hills a mile away move faster than mountains five miles away. This does not happen when I look straight ahead. The longer I can walk without taking my eyes off this side view, the further I can extend this enhanced sense of depth.

Eventually, I learn to walk gazing about in all directions as far as I can. My mind relaxes and expands as I walk through this vast, slowly changing view. My focus has spiraled far away from myself.

The World Expands

A MILE-WIDE GLACIER FLOWED past the base of my hill. From the glacier's other side rose a mountain that towered almost three miles above the glacier. Miles of intervening air tinted blue that enormous mountain's glory of shimmering white snow-fields and black rock cliffs.

No wind blew on that mid-September day. Birds had migrated. Ground squirrels were now hibernating. One fox passed by on its way to lower elevations. Stillness within a majestic setting.

Every fifteen or twenty minutes, though, I heard the gathering rumble of an avalanche. I scanned the mountain's slopes, for I dearly wanted to see enormous avalanches roaring down that mountain, but I could not see any. The sound lasted a long time, but search as I would, I couldn't see any trace of an avalanche. Time after time this happened, until I began to wonder if the sound came from something else.

Again I heard the rumble. Again I searched the mountain. And this time, I noticed a small cloud gently floating down the mountain far below the rumbling sound. As this "cloud" descended, it moved closer and grew louder, until it plunged over thousand-foot cliffs and collapsed on the glacier a mile away. The boom of that final collapse echoed within that basin of massive cliffs. The air throbbed long after the avalanching snow and ice lay still. The sound of an avalanche is a deep, low sound to begin with. As it echoes, the highest tones fade away first, so the sustained echo of that icy thunder reverberates at a lower and lower tone. Long after habit predicts the place should be quiet, the ear still hears a very deep sound, still perceptibly fading and deepening.

I learned to look lower on the mountain for something smaller than I had anticipated whenever I heard the beginning whoosh of an avalanche.

The avalanches were so far away that hundreds of tons of snow and ice plummeting a hundred miles per hour appeared as a little cloud floating gently down the mountain. Each avalanche was so many miles away that the sound I heard came from where the avalanche had been fifteen seconds earlier. During that fifteen-second gap, the avalanche had dropped a half-mile farther down the steep, snowy slopes. The actual avalanche was falling far below its noise. I had been looking too high.

I had overlooked the avalanches, because my eyes hadn't seen the true magnitude of a three-mile-tall mountain. A gap of distance separates me from the world I see. I bridge that gap by casting an assumption across it, but time after time I discover that my assumption is wrong and that I see the world smaller than it really is. Only when I take the time to calibrate my assumptions of distance do I see the world in its true, majestic size.

⌒

I sat under a tree on a Southwestern plateau, gazing across the void of a nearby canyon to where the plateau continued on the other side. While wondering how far away the opposite rim was, I realized that the pinyon pines over there probably grew to the same height as the pinyon pines growing over here. I compared myself to the trunks and branches of the trees around me and then looked at the trees on the other side. Their similar size allowed me to see how small a person over there would appear. With that human scale, the view suddenly became full of detail.

The pinyon pines on the other side grew on the slopes bordering a drainage. I looked around and discovered that I, too, was sitting on a slope above a dry streambed. I noticed a brown circular carpet of fallen pine needles beneath each nearby tree. When I looked across the canyon, I was amazed that I could see similar carpets beneath those distant trees. The distance had shrunk those ten-foot circles of brown needles to tiny details but they were clearly visible when I specifically looked for them.

The more I looked back and forth and interconnected the distant view with the land around me, the more each distant tree, rock, and drainage took on its proper proportion, until I saw that plateau with startling accuracy. I looked down like a hawk and saw myself within the patterns of this land. The land was dense with details of shape, texture, and size. The plateau was more spacious than I had realized. It extended through mile after mile of magical space.

GRADIENT OF DISTANCE

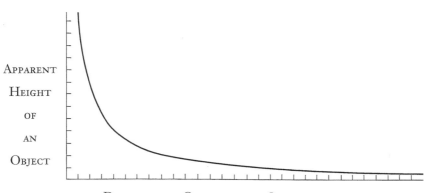

APPARENT
HEIGHT
OF
AN
OBJECT

DISTANCE OF OBJECT FROM OBSERVER

Everything appears smaller the further away it is. This is as true for our hand as it is for a galaxy. The rate of "shrinking" is mathematically simple. When an object is moved twice as far away, it appears half as large. This is true no matter what the scale. Something two miles (or two feet) away will appear half the size it did when it was one mile (or one foot) away. Every time the distance is doubled, the apparent size is cut in half. This leads to the above graph of apparent size as seen from various distances.

Though the same mathematical pattern of shrinking holds true throughout this graph, the shrinking "feels" different at different distances. We are most familiar with the world close at hand (the left side of the graph). As the plunging line shows, objects "shrink" quickly within that part of the world we can reach out and touch. A simple movement from one foot away to two feet away cuts the apparent size in half.

However, the vast majority of the world we see lies "out there" in the almost-flat line, right-hand-side of the graph. Out there, visual "shrinking" becomes subtle. Something five miles away will appear almost the same size as something four miles away. In the distant world that we see but cannot touch, tiny changes in size express large changes in distance. If we apply the visual assumptions we've learned from the world right around us to the larger world, we will overlook these subtle changes; the distant world flattens into backdrop scenery. But if we learn to pay attention to these subtle details, the distant world expands into vastness.

A similar thing happens when I walk with friends. The human figure is a powerful visual measuring stick. My brain automatically uses the human figure, when available, to judge the size of the world around me. If I always hike close to my companions, their bodies will always appear large, which will make the surrounding world seem smaller by comparison. But if I drop behind occasionally, my companions appear smaller and I notice larger patterns. The greater the distance between us, the more accurately their bodies reveal the true size of the land we walk within.

⌇

Patterns fill the world with details. Different distances reveal different patterns. A tundra beetle leads me to tiny patterns of dropped seeds and lain eggs. Close by are small, human-scale patterns. In the distance are larger patterns of rock layers, drainages, and vegetation. Usually I overlook these distant patterns; I lump them together into "out there." This makes sense in terms of survival because distant things usually pose little danger.

However, if I take the time, I can interconnect near and distant patterns by shifting my focus back and forth between them. Nearby patterns give meaning to distant details, which help reveal patterns too large to notice right around me.

⌇

Shifting back and forth between a distant view and the immediate world becomes a technique for seeing more. While gazing from a mountain ridge one day, I noticed that distant clouds had flat bottoms. This was easy to see because I was seeing the distant clouds from the side. The flat bottom of a cloud marks the shifting point along an upward gradient of cooling air at which water vapor condenses into a cloud. The more flat bottoms I noticed, the more easily I could see that they all "rested" on a layer extending smoothly through the atmosphere above me. My eyes could extend this layer through more distant cloud bottoms until they disappeared behind the horizon. Beyond those clouds could be seen just the tops of even more distant clouds. The layer curved over the horizon.

I cannot see the curve of the solid Earth from the ground because that curve hides behind the horizon it creates. But I can see the curving, cloud-marked layer of the transparent atmosphere embracing our planet. Its curve simultaneously reveals two seemingly contradictory truths. The Earth is vast, far larger than I am usually aware of. There is so much room for the human spirit on this planet. But the Earth is also finite. A straight line can extend forever but the curve of the Earth will curve back on itself. A straight horizon can imply resources extending forever. A curved horizon declares that all of our resources are finite. Together, these two truths make the Earth so precious. Like the atmosphere, I can reach out and embrace the planet although my arms won't reach all the way around.

Sitting

⌣

I STOP WALKING AND SUDDENLY NOTICE that all the clouds are drifting overhead. While I was moving, my motion had obscured their slow, steady passage.

After driving many miles, I stop and get out to stretch. After listening to road noise for an hour, my ears hear nothing. Yet that is different than hearing the quiet. If I wait, I soon hear a nearby bird singing. Later, I can hear a gust of wind touching the slope above. Then I hear the song of a bird down by the stream and then the murmur of the brook itself. After several minutes, I am finally hearing the gentle sounds that compose quiet. It has taken time for my ears to open to the quiet. This time of adjustment reminds me of walking into a dark theater; I can see nothing at first. If I wait, however, my eyes dilate and a world previously hidden by darkness becomes visible.

⌣

Once, while I sat observing ducks in a marsh, a weasel popped out of a hole near my feet. It held a slain baby mouse in its mouth. The weasel stood there, uncertain whether to retreat into the hole or carry off its booty. While I had been quietly sitting, a murder was perpetrated in dark tunnels beneath me. Another time, while I was lying on a tundra ridge gazing at the sky, a wheatear (an Arctic bird) twice tried to land on my knees because they were the highest perch around. Another time, while I watched a deer carcass in the desert, two black-tailed rattlesnakes flowed out of a nearby bush. By pushing against each other, they raised their twined bodies straight up into the air, then curved back onto the ground, pushed again up into the air, curved back down, and flowed away into the bushes. Animals will approach me more closely while I'm sitting than I can approach a sitting animal.

⌁

I took kids to explore tidepools. After exploring with them for an hour, I sought an out-of-the-way tidepool to see what I might see if I sat quietly. Several sunny minutes passed. A quick, brief movement on a nearby boulder caught my attention out of the corner of my eye. "Flies buzzing," I thought and turned back to the tidepools. However, the brief movements kept drawing my eye back to that boulder. I finally walked over to the distracting rock and sat down to confirm the presence of flies. No flies. I waited. A minute later, I saw the movement again—yet I could see nothing. Movement again. It was as if the plants themselves moved. Again! I looked more closely and saw a very small crab. As I watched, another one moved. Then another and another.

The crabs emerged out of crannies hidden beneath the seaweed that covered the boulder. Bits of plants cloaked the back of each crab. This camouflage explained why I had seen only movements. The tidepools were full of "invisible" animals lying camouflaged in hidden crannies, waiting until all was quiet to emerge, scuttling sideways.

I wanted the students to experience how a tidepool can come to life when one sits quietly, so I called some kids over, telling them I had found something neat. As the kids approached, the crabs scuttled back into their crevices and crannies. I explained that there were crabs on the rock and if we sat quietly long enough, a lot of crabs would come out.

We sat for a time. Just when the crabs were beginning to stir, another kid came up. The crabs retreated. "What are you guys watching?" I explained, and we all started waiting again. One of the kids got bored and stretched. His movement scared the crabs back into their crannies. We started over again. The group was growing restless now. They had been sitting for what seemed a long time and had seen nothing. Meanwhile, there were tidepools all around to explore. A child got up and left and we had to start all over again. I never was able to show the crabs to any of the kids. The crabs remained invisible to them.

⌁

The kids reminded me of what I was like when I began backpacking. By walking, I surrounded myself with change. The air whispered past my ears. Birds flew and animals bounded away. The unknown world over the next rise drew me on and on.

When I stopped, all this change stopped. I was surrounded by stillness. Nothing seemed to be happening. Why should I waste my time sitting in this boring place when I could keep walking and seeing new things? I took rest stops only because my body needed them. Yet as I sat propped against my pack, sipping water from my canteen, resting, animals adjusted to my presence. Bees settled back onto the flowers. Birds returned to high perches and resumed singing. Lizards crawled back onto their sunning rocks.

These animals drew my focus to overlooked details. Details dissolved edges into interconnected gradients. As I focused on the details within gradients, I saw stages of various processes. I began to look around for intermediate stages of these processes. As my focus moved back and forth through the distances, the different distances fused into a wondrously vast space extending smoothly in all directions.

I gazed into this magic space at distant details that were part of patterns too large for me to notice right around me. Large patterns revealed stages of immense geological and ecological processes. Over the centuries, these slow changes accumulate the power to shape the Earth. Slow, ongoing changes are difficult to detect because there are no beginnings, no jerkiness, no endings to catch my attention. But the longer I sat, the more slow changes I noticed, until the vast landscape vibrated with change.

My awareness of this place had increased through a spiral of change. A sharpening focus had led to greater understanding and greater understanding had sharpened my focus. As my eyes opened to the vastness, the seemingly boring place in which I began my rest transformed into a special place full of life, space, and stately change.

Over many years of hiking, my rest stops have become longer, until I now find myself hiking in order to find a quiet place to sit for a long time. I sit, and as my mind quietly explores the view, a rigid world of objects melts into a flowing world of change. I practice seeing a world of merging gradients rather than of separating edges; a world swirling with spirals of change rather than simple causes and effects. Within this flowing world, I encounter again and again the two levels and the Rule of Flow.

The Two Levels

I STOPPED FOR LUNCH BY A MOUNTAIN STREAM. Throughout lunch, I digested the beauty of the freshly fallen snow on the overhanging branches while I gazed at the splashing confusion of drops and pools, cascades and eddies within the rushing stream. I idly tossed in a stick. The moment my eyes focused on the floating stick, the stream appeared to move more slowly than before. I tossed in another stick. Its journey was easy to follow. The stick slowed as it approached a pool that formed upstream of a maze of rocks. The stick drifted across the pool, accelerated through a chute between the rocks, and then tumbled about when the rushing water tripped over the slow water in the deep pool below.

I threw sticks into different parts of the stream and discovered the fascinating diversity of paths by which water moved through that stream. The smaller the stick, the slower it appeared to move and the more patterns it revealed within the seemingly chaotic stream. I played with seeing how small a stick I could follow with my eyes. What would I see if I could follow a water molecule down the stream?

As I watched each stick, I clearly heard the sound coming from each specific place through which the stick passed: the quiet of a pool, the throbbing of a drop-off, the hissing of bubbles surfacing in the plunge pool beneath. The stream's noise gradually resolved into a symphony of a hundred different sounds played by a hundred different places within the stream.

Initially, I had been gazing simply at the "stream," listening to its overall sound. But each stick shifted my focus to a specific "piece" of water flowing within the stream. That shift in focus changed what I heard and saw.

All morning we hiked down a desert canyon. As the day's heat intensified, we stopped in the shade beneath a cottonwood tree. On the canyon wall above, water from a spring flowed down a steep rock channel smoothed by many centuries of flowing water. Interestingly, the flow of water ended halfway down the slope. The water must have been evaporating as it flowed down the warm rock. The stream of evaporating water became thinner and thinner until it simply ended partway down the slope.

The day grew hotter and the water evaporated faster. The stream could not flow as far. The end of the stream receded up the slope. The afternoon heat finally subsided into the warmth of late afternoon. Now the stream could flow farther before all of its water evaporated. The end of the stream advanced down the slope. During the night, the stream would be able to flow all the way down into the sandy floor of the canyon. The next day, the end of the stream would rise again out of the sand and ascend the cliff. Like a thermometer, the lower end of the stream would rise and fall with the temperature.

The end of the stream can recede up the slope even though the water within the stream always flows down the slope. The stream and the water within the stream are two different things. They can behave differently.

If an accident occurs on a freeway, traffic will " back up" even though none of the individual cars actually shift into reverse and back up. If I focus on individual cars, I see them slowing down but continuing to move forward. However, if I focus on the flow of traffic, I see a place where the brake lights go on and I can almost hear the drivers swear. That " swearing place" does move "upstream," farther and farther from the accident. I notice different things within the flow depending upon where I focus.

Seeing the two different kinds of behaviors within a flow is important to the story in this book so I will give them names. I can focus on the "individual level" (of cars or drops of water) and watch how these individuals move. Or I can focus on the " group level" (of traffic or a stream) and watch the overall appearance created by the combined movements of all the individuals. Which level I focus on determines what I see.

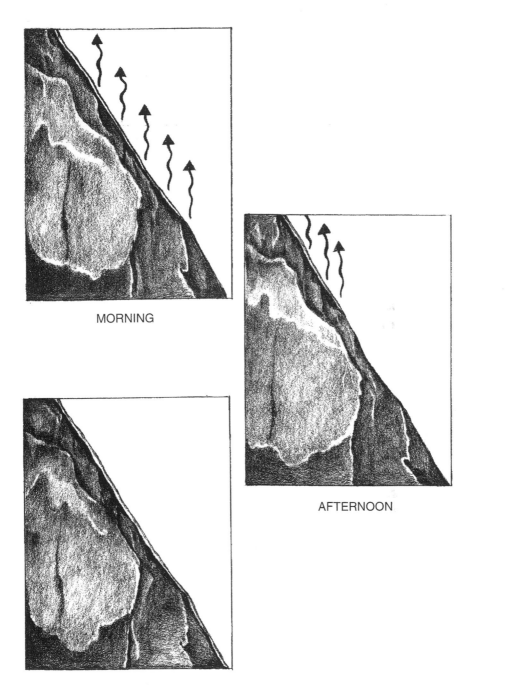

MORNING

AFTERNOON

EVENING

Like a thermometer, the end of the seep rises and falls with the temperature.

Mid-September. Late autumn in the foothills of the Alaskan Range. Red and brown leaves on the low tundra plants. Freezing nights. I am sitting quietly in geological thought. I grow vaguely aware of bird calls downslope. A snow bunting lands near me. Then another and another. I look around. Downslope, the tundra is covered with hundreds of foraging snow buntings. Other buntings are flying over them and landing all around me. Soon I am surrounded by chirping snow buntings busily foraging. Birds from somewhere downslope fly just over my head in a small but steady flow and land at the head of the foraging flock, so that more and more birds hop about upslope of me.

Eventually, the downslope end of the flock comes into sight. I can see that the birds flying overhead to the front of the flock are coming from the back edge of the flock. When these birds fly up from the back, the birds that are foraging ahead of them become the new back edge of the flock. They in turn fly forward. This behavior creates a steady stream of birds flying from the back of the flock to the front, which is now far upslope of me.

The flock forms a great wheel, rolling south over the tundra.

The flock flows over the land. By shifting my focus between the two different levels of flow, I see two different but equally wonderful behaviors. When I focus on the individual level, on individual snow buntings within the flock, I see each bird able to devote five minutes to foraging securely in the middle of a thousand chirping birds. When the bird notices that it is at the back edge of the flock and no longer protected, it takes a quick half-minute flight up to the head of the flock. Within seconds, it is again surrounded and can resume its search for food.

When I focus on the group level of the flow, I see the flock as a great wheel rolling south over the tundra. The back of the flock rolls up and over the flock on the ground and touches down ahead of it. This flow guarantees that each bird won't land on an area already harvested by another member of the flock. The rolling of the flock never stops, for the season is late. The flock doesn't move as fast as individual birds could fly but it remains in motion even as each bird is given the opportunity and protection to rest and feed on the sparse harvest of the late-Autumn tundra.

The back end of the flock reaches me. A few stragglers, intent on foraging, hop about. One looks up, sees it is no longer in the protection of the flock, gives a startled call, and flies upslope toward the front of the flock. The other stragglers hear the call and fly away. The foraging flock rolls away up the slope. The thousand chirps recede, leaving me behind in the vast stillness.

The Rule of Flow

I F I T U R N T H E W A T E R O N F U L L B L A S T so that it pours into the sink faster than it drains away, the water level rises. If I turn the water down so that it drains away faster than it pours in, the water level drops.

At rush hour, more cars enter the freeways than exit. Traffic accumulates. Rush hour subsides as more cars exit the freeways than enter.

Dust is so tiny that it almost floats in air. It takes hours for dust to settle in absolutely calm air and the slightest drafts, which homes are full of, keep the dust particles stirred up. Some of this dust drifts under the bed, where the air is calm enough for some of the dust to settle. Not as much dust drifts out as drifted in, so balls of dust gradually grow beneath the bed.

Water swirls out from a stream's main current, circles in an eddy, and flows beneath the surface back to the main current. Floating things, however, cannot follow the underwater path out of the eddy. Sticks, leaves, and dead bugs floating on the water can flow into the eddy but they can't flow out, so they gather within the eddy. Each eddy inevitably accumulates a spinning "raft" of debris.

The Rule of Flow connects the two levels within any flow. The Rule of Flow is this:

> **Inflow greater than outflow causes an accumulation at the group level.**
> *If I earn dollars (individual level) faster than I spend them, my bank account (group level) increases.*

Inflow less than outflow causes a reduction at the group level.
If I wash clothes (individual level) faster than they get dirty, the laundry pile (group level) diminishes.

If inflow is equal to outflow, the group level remains steady.
If I exercise and burn up calories (individual level) as fast as I eat them, my weight (group level) remains constant.

The balance between inflow and outflow determines what happens on the group level. If I make a million dollars per day, my bank account will still dwindle if I spend two million dollars per day. If I reduce living expenses to twenty cents per week, my bank account will still dwindle if I make only ten cents a week. The balance is relative.

A change in either inflow or outflow can shift the relative balance, causing the group level to change in a new direction. Lines form in grocery stores when shoppers flow to the check-out stands faster than they can be checked out. When the lines grow too long, another check-out stand is opened. Outflow increases. If the outflow becomes greater than inflow, the lines will shorten. Agencies that lack competition often won't open another window even when their lines are enormously long, as many drivers seeking to renew their licenses have experienced.

Reducing outflow has the same effect on the relative balance as increasing inflow. When I am cold, I can turn up the heat or put on a jacket. A well-insulated jacket warms me not by increasing the flow of heat to my body but by reducing the flow of heat away from my body. This shifts the relative balance. Heat (individual level) flowing away from me starts to accumulate beneath the jacket and the temperature (group level) next to my body rises. Its like getting into a shower in which the water is too cold. I tend to automatically turn up the hot water. But I can also warm the shower by turning down the cold water. There is always more than one way to shift a relative balance.

༺

The Rule of Flow might seem simplistically obvious when applied to situations with which we are familiar, but it helps me notice flows that I would otherwise overlook. For example, male deer, moose, and elk grow a pair of antlers each year. The antlers reach full size by autumn. After

Why the world is not buried beneath fallen antlers.

the mating season, the antlers drop off. A new set of antlers develops the following spring.

The Rule of Flow prepares my mind to see the antlers as an inflow onto the ground each autumn. But the fallen antlers don't accumulate century after century until the land is covered by an impenetrable thicket of fallen antlers. Somehow the antlers flow away from the forest floor at the same annual rate they enter. But how?

Occasionally I find stumps of antler among the spruce cones of a squirrel's midden pile. Tiny gnaw marks etch the remaining bits of antler. These clues reveal what is happening to the antlers. Rodents eat them. Fallen antlers (and bones) are a winter source of calcium and phosphorous for many animals. All through the winter, antlers flow from the forest floor into rodents.

The flow doesn't stop in the rodents, either. The rodents defecate, eventually die. The minerals from their bodies dissolve into the soil, where plants absorb them and use them to grow new leaves. All summer, the deer eat the leaves. Some of the minerals accumulate within the growing new antlers.

I once saw antlers as just antlers, but now I perceive them as an accumulation on the group level of minerals flowing through soil, plants, deer, and rodents. The Rule of Flow helps me connect parts of the world that I previously saw as separate.

⌒

Sometimes, outflow is easier to notice than inflow. I rafted down an Arctic river one summer. Each evening, I camped on one of its many islands. The islands had fewer mosquitoes than the shore and I hoped they also had fewer bears.

Each island had a similar form that made choosing a landing and camping site easy. A sandy beach, perfect for camping, formed the rounded upstream end of each island. I simply drifted down upon the island until my boat gently beached. Then I jumped onto the sand and pulled my boat ashore to a fine campsite. I tried to explore these forested islands, but I couldn't penetrate the dense thicket of willow and young spruce trees that separated the open beach from the forest beyond.

I couldn't land anywhere else, because downstream of the beach the shores grew increasingly steep. High, undercut banks formed the down-

The island moves upstream, although the sand within it always moves downstream.

stream end of each island. Chunks of undercut bank frequently fell into the river. I heard several ker-plops each time I floated past the lower end of an island. Withered roots of trees stuck out of these eroding banks. Trees near the undercut banks were at various stages of toppling into the river. Some trees were leaning toward the edge while others had fallen and were sticking straight out above the river. A few trees had dropped into the water but their roots still held them to the island.

The banks were eroding fast enough to remove these islands within a few centuries. Yet it didn't make sense that all the islands in this river would soon disappear. Surely the river would continue to have islands. But in order to maintain the islands, there had to be an inflow of material large enough to balance the outflow from eroding banks. Where was the inflow?

Each island I drifted by had a similar gradient of vegetation growing from its upstream end to its downstream end. A bare sandy beach at the upper end was followed by willow seedlings, then a willow thicket, then a willow thicket with young spruce trees growing out of it, then a young spruce forest, and finally an older spruce forest at the downstream end. Drifting past this gradient of vegetation was like drifting through time and watching the process (called succession) by which a spruce forest becomes established on bare sand.

A spruce tree would not grow well on the sunny, open beach, because a spruce seedling grows best in the shade. Willows, however, thrive in moist, open areas. They quickly cover the open sand with a thicket. This thicket will trap more sand from each spring's high floodwaters. The trapped sand will raise the surface of the island beneath the willows. The willows also cover the ground with their shade. Now spruce seedlings can grow there. As they rise above the thicket, the spruce trees shade the willows and the willows gradually die. A young spruce forest replaces the aging willow thicket.

The island's upper end is just being colonized by plants, while the lower end has a well-established, centuries-old forest. The upstream end of the island must be younger than the downstream end. This gradient of age reveals the inflow that sustains these islands. The young beach is a fresh deposit of sand. The river deposits sand on the upstream end of the island and carries away sand (and the trees that have grown upon it) from the downstream end. The island grows at its head and diminishes at its foot.

But this means that the island is migrating upstream like a geologic salmon! The island moves upstream, although the individual sand grains within it always move downstream. Grains of sand may stop upon the island to rest for a few centuries, but eventually they drop back into the river and continue on their journey to the sea. The island is the group level of flow; the sand that composes it is the individual level. They move in opposite directions. Over several centuries, my sandy campsite at the head of the island will become the forest falling into the river at the foot of the island.

Invisible Flows

I ENJOY BUILDING A SAND DAM across the tiny stream flowing across the beach. Downstream of my dam, the water flows away. The stream fades into the sand. Upstream of my dam, the water flows into a deepening pool. This pool rises until it begins flowing around the end of my dam. I heap beach sand to lengthen the dam. The pool keeps filling and soon the rising pool threatens to overflow the dam. I build the dam higher. The pool grows deeper. My thin dam was adequate when the pool level was low but as the pool rises, it exerts greater pressure against the dam. The dam begins to bulge. I thicken and reinforce the dam. While I do this, the pool expands enough to start flowing around the dam. I must lengthen the dam again.

My dam must grow taller to hold back the rising water. My dam must lengthen to confine the expanding pool. My dam must thicken to resist the increasing pressure. I can keep this game up for some time, but eventually the increasing pressure of the deepening pool will force water through the dam. The liquefying sand begins to ooze. A section sags. The pent-up pool surges through the breach and the dam washes away.

My dam interrupted the balanced flow of the tiny stream. Upstream of the dam, inflow became greater than outflow and water accumulated. The more water that accumulated, the harder it became to maintain the dam.

Snowshoe hares filled the spruce forests the first summer I visited Alaska. I could stop anywhere and see ten or fifteen "rabbits" around me, even in the middle of the day. I could approach astonishingly close to them. They had stripped the lower branches from all the plants.

For many years, the births of hares had been greater than the deaths of hares. The number of hares (individual level) flowing from birth to death accumulated and the population (group level) increased. But that winter, their population crashed. When I returned the next year, I saw only three snowshoe hares the entire summer! In less than a year, the relative balance between hare births and hare deaths had shifted dramatically.

Many things had caused this drastic shift. The hares had been so abundant that they were always foraging close to one another. This constant closeness created stress. The stripped plants of summer meant less forage for the oncoming long winter. Stressed, starving bodies succumb to disease. Because the animals were living so close together, diseases could pass quickly through the population. In addition, more predators now hunted the hares, because owls and lynxes had been able to raise many babies during the recent years of abundant prey.

The population crash changed all these factors. Now, the few surviving hares were no longer stressed or contagious. The predators would starve and diminish. The plants could grow faster than they were cropped. The relative balance between births and deaths could shift and the population would increase once again. In about ten years, the snowshoe hare population will grow too dense, the relative balance will shift again, and the population will crash.

⌒

When I was a child, I pulled my sled for half an hour to reach the tallest sledding hill in town. I went up and down that hill all afternoon, until the few remaining sledders were dark shadows, more easily heard than seen in the growing dusk. Finally, I trudged wearily home through the dark to a snack, a hot bath, and a warm dinner.

I visited that hill recently. The biggest change was that most of the kids had been driven to the hill. A lot of cars and adults stood around while the kids sledded. Now, one would expect the result of this change to be more sledding time, because a child no longer has to spend a precious hour walking from home and back again. But that was not the result. The parents were getting cold standing around. Within half an hour, they were telling their protesting children that it was time to get in the car and go home.

Winter cold creates a large outflow of heat from the body. The kids stayed warm by walking up the sledding hill over and over again. This climbing generated enough heat to balance winter's large outflow of heat. But the parents just stood around, while an unbalanced outflow of heat made them colder and colder. All too soon, they had to go home.

Imbalances are hard to maintain. This is true of any flow. The kids' balanced heat flow allowed them to sled all day, but the adults could not tolerate their unbalanced heat flow for very long. As the snowshoe hares' population grew, the pressures of disease, starvation, and predation increased, until finally the expanding population flowed away in one winter. My dam survived only a few minutes, while the unimpeded beach stream could flow for centuries. Unbalanced flows are unstable; they must adjust or soon disappear. Balanced flows can endure; the world gradually fills with balanced flows.

⌒

Balanced flows, however, can be deceptive. A balanced flow is one where inflow equals outflow. Therefore, the group level does not change. The only change occurs on the individual level. If the flow of individuals is obvious (as it is with water or cars), then the flow is easily visible. But if the individual particles are very tiny (such as the exhalation of gases into the atmosphere from termites hidden within logs) or if the flow is very slow (such as the creep of soil down a slope), then the flow within the individual level will not be noticed. Nothing will seem to be changing.

Such flows are invisible. I might be surrounded by balanced flows and yet be unaware of them. I will notice only the unchanging group level and assume that is the way things are always meant to be. I will treat this invisible, balanced flow as if it were a dependable certainty. If I unwittingly alter this invisible flow by shifting the relative balance, the "way things are always meant to be" will begin flowing away. Most of our environmental problems are examples of taken-for-granted certainties changing in unexpected ways.

Beaches, for example, have existed throughout history. They seem to be a fixed certainty. Yet if I throw a stick into the breakers, I can watch the waves push the stick not only in and out from the beach, but also relentlessly down the coast. Waves do the same thing to the sand. Beach sand is constantly being carried slowly down along the coast. A beach is the group level expression of a flow of trillions of sand grains along the coast. Beaches would disappear without an inflow of sand to replace the outflow. Rivers supply the new sand. Every river transports rocks from the mountains of its headwaters. By the time these rocks reach the ocean, they have been crumbled and tumbled into mostly sand. But this sand flows along the bottom of rivers, out of sight.

If we build dams across these rivers, this invisible flow of sand will accumulate behind the dams, because sand cannot flow over the dams. The flow of sand to the beaches is interrupted. The relative balance shifts, sand flows away from the beaches faster than it is replenished, and the beaches diminish. Owners of beachfront property wonder why something that has been here throughout history can suddenly begin to disappear. Nature seems quirky or malevolent.

⌐⌐

A diversity of nutritious grasses grow on grasslands. People see this unchanging range as a given resource that can feed more animals. They bring in more cattle and keep them there too long. These cattle naturally avoid plants that are bitter or covered with thorns; they prefer to eat plants that are tasty and nutritious. The cattle eat the nutritious plants faster than the plants can grow. The populations of nutritious species decline, leaving the range wide open to the species the cattle avoid (such as cactus). The cattlemen speak of the cactus as "invading" the once-productive grassland, as if the degradation was the fault of the cactus.

⌐⌐

The threat of the "greenhouse effect" stems from a series of shifts in the relative balances of many invisible flows. Our atmosphere is the group level expression of many massive yet balanced flows of invisible gases. Gases flow into the atmosphere as fast as they flow out of the atmosphere. Our technology, however, has increased the flow of carbon dioxide into the atmosphere, thereby shifting this relative balance toward accumulation. This shift in gas composition shifts the relative balance of global energy flow because carbon dioxide strongly absorbs the wavelengths at which energy radiates out through the Earth's atmosphere— much more than it absorbs the wavelengths at which energy radiation enters the Earth's atmosphere. Therefore, an increase in carbon dioxide increases the amount of solar energy that stays in the Earth's atmosphere. Such a shift would cause an increase in the Earth's average temperature. This warming might increase the melting of icecaps. If meltwater flows into the ocean faster than water evaporates out of the ocean, sea levels will rise. Many cities would be flooded. The atmosphere, the Earth's temperature, ice caps, and sea level are all group level expressions of invisible flows. These things that we take for granted will remain constant only if their underlying flows remain balanced.

Usually I see the world only at the group level of flow. At this level, the world appears full of unchanging things I take for granted. But detecting invisible flows is an enjoyable game and as I practice, my world transforms into vast swirling flows. Continents flow back into the sea, gases flow through the atmosphere, and molecules flow through my body. Balanced, invisible flows might underlie anything I take for granted. The "balance of nature" is profoundly more true than I once realized.

Time Lags

~~

MY WIFE ALYSIA WISELY INCLUDED a cup and pitcher among the bathtub toys of our daughters when they were toddlers. The bathtub is a better place than the dinner table to learn about pouring and filling.

Pouring into a cup is baffling for toddlers. They pour their liquid into the cup until it reaches the full mark. Then they tip the pitcher back. But the cup overflows! It happens over and over again in the most confounding way. They are receiving their first introduction to the confusion of time lags.

One time lag occurs between when they start tipping the pitcher back and when liquid stops flowing out of it. A second time lag comes between when liquid flows out of the pitcher and when it flows into the cup. These two times lags guarantee that a child's first attempt to fill a cup will create an overflow. To properly fill a cup, one must start tilting the pitcher back up before the cup is full.

~~

Another classic grappling with time lags is steering a car. Why do we start turning the steering wheel to the left when we are in the middle of our turn to the right? Until we master this "contradictory" logic, some frantic swerving can occur. A detailed analysis of this swerving can help us better understand the confusing dynamics of time lags.

Using the illustration on the facing page, let's begin with a car that is curving too far to the left (1). The front tires are turned to the left and the car is beginning to cross the center line. I start to turn the steering wheel to the right, but the car keeps turning to the left (2). This is because it takes time for the front tires to swivel from their left-heading position over to a right-heading position. Though their heading is *turning toward* the right, it is still angled toward the left, so the car itself continues to turn to the left. Frantically, I turn the steering wheel harder to the right.

The front tires continue to swivel to the right until their heading is straight ahead (3). The car no longer turns; it hurtles along a straight line now, but this straight line is heading off the road to the left. Frantically, I turn the steering wheel harder to the right.

Finally, the front tires have swiveled enough to point them toward the right (4). Finally, the car starts to turn to the right. In terms of the road, however, the car is *still* drifting to the left, because—just as with the front wheels that preceded them—it takes time for the car to change from a left-heading direction to a right-heading direction. During this time, even though the car's heading is *turning toward* the right, it is still angled toward the left and the car itself continues to move to the left. The car moves to the left as it turns to the right. (Confused? Now you can understand why toddlers keep overflowing their cups.) Frantically, I turn the steering wheel harder to the right.

The car continues to turn to the right until its heading is finally

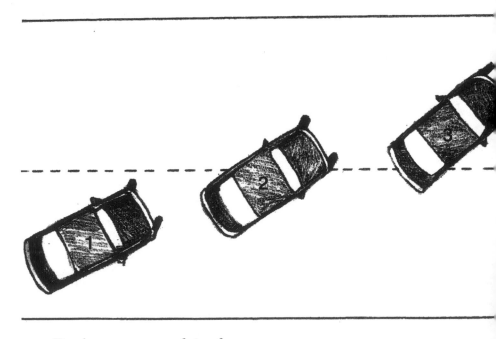

Time lags can create a confusion of swerves.

aligned with the road (5). The car stops drifting to the left. At this point, even though the steering wheel is turned very hard to the right and the front tires are swiveled hard to the right and the car is turning right, the car has reached the left-most part of its swerve. And the car is way over on the left side of the road. Frantically, I turn the steering wheel harder to the right, desperate to get the car back on the right side of the road. (Unless there is oncoming traffic, an experienced driver would now start to turn the steering wheel to the left.)

The car is turning very fast to the right by now (6). By the time it comes across the center line, the car is heading off the road to the right. Frantically, I turn the steering wheel hard to the left. The whole process of swerving in one direction turns into the process of swerving back in the other direction.

I encounter the same confusing logic when I interact with flows (of which the world is invisibly full). All the hiking books say to carry a gallon of water when hiking in the desert, so I made sure I lugged this eight

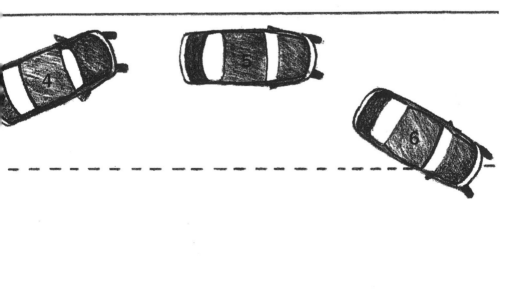

pounds of water with me. I started hiking at sunrise. By midday, the Sun was overhead, beating down hot. The day was half over, I had hiked more than half of my distance easily, and I had only gone through one quart of water. I started to think I must by a better hiker than the fuddy-duddy literature assumed, and started to think I wouldn't carry so much water next time.

I hiked on. The day grew hotter and hotter. I went through my second quart. The temperature was growing too hot for walking. I found some shade and went through my third quart as I simply sat out the full heat of day. I started to worry that I had not brought enough water. The late afternoon temperature began to back off and I began to hike again. My water needs declined and I still had a bit of water as I cruised easily through the gathering cool of evening to my destination.

Since I had drunk only one quart in the first half of the day, I had assumed I would drink only two quarts during the entire day. I did not understand the time lag involved in the daily temperature. The hottest part of the day is not at midday, even though the Sun is overhead and the most intense at that time. The hottest part of the day is several hours later.

This temperature time lag occurs because of a confusing relationship between the two levels of heat flow to the Earth: heat (individual level) and temperature (group level). Heat from the Earth flows out to the cold vacuum of space at a fairly steady rate. However, the inflow of the heat from the Sun fluctuates from night to day. All night, the outflow of heat is greater than the inflow of heat, so the amount of heat in the night shaded part of the Earth diminishes. The temperature declines. When our region turns back into the sunlight, heat energy again flows onto the land. As we keep turning toward the Sun, the inflow of heat energy increases. At some point (usually shortly after "sunrise"), the increasing inflow of heat becomes greater than the outflow of heat and the temperature begins to rise.

We face the Sun most directly at midday. The greatest amount of energy is now flowing onto this part of the Earth. So midday represents the maximum inflow of heat (individual level). The inflow of heat is so much greater than the outflow of heat at this time that the level of heat, that is, the temperature, is rising rapidly.

After midday, the inflow of heat starts to decline. Throughout the afternoon, as we turn away from the Sun, the inflow of heat declines from its midday maximum. However, as long as this inflow remains greater than the outflow, heat will continue to accumulate, lifting the temperature still higher. Throughout the afternoon, the two levels of heat flow are changing in opposite directions. The temperature continues to rise even as the underlying inflow of heat declines. Not until the declining inflow of heat becomes less than the outflow of heat will the temperature rise level out and then begin to decline. That shifting point doesn't happen until many hours after midday. So the maximum temperature occurs many hours after the maximum inflow of heat.

⌒

A similar confusing time lag happens on an annual cycle. The longest day of the year (in the Northern Hemisphere), June 21, has the greatest inflow of heat. After June 21, the amount of heat flowing in each day declines, because the days grow shorter and the sunlight enters the atmosphere at a lower angle. However, this declining rate of inflow is still far greater than the rate at which heat flows away from the Northern Hemisphere. Therefore, heat continues to accumulate. Finally, after many weeks of shortening days, there comes a time when the inflow of solar energy has diminished to the point where all it can do is balance the outflow of heat. That marks the hottest days, usually in the dog days of August or early September. Only then do the temperatures begin to decline.

Similarly, December 21 is the shortest day of the year. The least amount of solar energy flows into our hemisphere on this day. The average temperature is in its steepest decline. Thereafter, more energy enters during the increasingly long days. But until the daily increase in energy grows large enough to balance the outflow of energy, the daily temperature will keep dropping. Only after several weeks of lengthening days does the day get long enough for enough energy to enter the hemisphere to counterbalance the outflow of heat. It is at that point that we experience the coldest temperatures, usually in February, a time when the growing daylength is apparent to all.

One time lag can underlie another time lag. The amount of snow on the ground is determined by the relative balance between snow falling and snow melting. Snow will accumulate only when the temperature is below a certain level. In many places, snow hasn't even fallen by December 21, the shortest day of the year, because the temperature is not yet cold enough. But as the temperature continues to drop, the snow begins to accumulate. It continues to accumulate as long as the temperature stays cold enough. During the coldest days of February, great amounts of snow will accumulate. But for many weeks thereafter, as the temperature begins to rise, the average temperature continues to be cold enough for snow to accumulate. In these places, the maximum amount of snow will occur in March or April—a time lag of several weeks from the coldest days of February, which lagged several weeks behind the shortest days of December.

~

Clarifying the confusion of time lags requires precise distinctions. There is a significant distinction between "short days" and "days growing shorter." The days of January are short days, though they are growing longer every day. The days of July are long days, but they are growing shorter every day. The days of November are short days that are growing even shorter every day. Similarly, understanding how a car can still be moving toward the left when the wheels are turned to the right requires being precise in distinguishing the heading of the road, the heading of the car, and the heading of the tires. In our national government, we must be precise in distinguishing between "reducing the debt" and "reducing the deficit." The first phrase means moving out of debt. The second phrase means slowing down the rate at which one moves ever further into debt. There is a difference.

Time lags make it difficult for us to understand how changes in underlying flows create changes in the world we see. Because the world is so full of invisible flows with their relative balances and different levels, the world is also unfortunately full of invisible confusions—thanks to time lags. We became especially confused when the two levels are moving in opposite directions. Then it's easy to slip into thinking that the two levels are disconnected, that the declines (or increases) at the lower level have no bearing on the accumulations (or declines) on the upper level. As long as we still find plenty of food in the supermarket, concerns about a global collapse in fisheries or mite infestations eliminating honeybees and much of our agricultural pollination can appear academic. If we do not understand time lags, we will ignore these imbalances in the underlying levels. For example, some people don't want to require changes in emissions until scientists can document harm coming from the "greenhouse effect." By that time, it may be too late to reverse the effect.

The confusion created by two levels moving in opposite directions is most intense near a "peak." By the time the swerving car reaches its leftmost position on the road, for example, it is already turning strongly to the right. Is it moving to the left or to the right? That depends upon what level of its motion I analyze. Or imagine a person becoming prodigal with a large source of income. As long as income exceeds expenses, the person's financial worth will increase. If the person grows more lavish and wasteful, expenses eventually will surpass income. Right at that point, the person's financial worth will be greatest. From that point on, financial worth will decline. At the group level, this is a high point, the peak. At the individual level, this is a turning point, the beginning of a decline. Similarly, an historical peak in a nation's wealth and influence can be seen as the crescendo of their Golden Age—or as that point when a history of increasingly bad decisions or events finally overtook their inflow of wealth.

These areas of confusion make me philosophical, because our history is filled with so many rises and collapses of civilizations that it feels like a car swerving back and forth against a guardrail. Perhaps we humans are beginners at the wheel of a recent creation called culture who haven't yet learned that we need to turn out of a swerve earlier than we think.

I contemplate time lags a lot. Because they occur everywhere, I find that the lessons I draw spill richly into all areas of my life. For example, if I try to improve a deteriorating situation, I should be prepared psychologically for the situation to first get worse. This does not mean that my actions are futile. It just means it takes time to reverse momentum. Things have to get worse before they get better. Instead of becoming discouraged, I should focus on whether the deterioration is slowing down.

On the other hand, this also means I shouldn't wait too long to try to improve something. By then, the momentum might carry things beyond my power to turn. One of the lessons of the swerving car is that the sooner I begin to correct, the less sharply I have to turn.

But the main lesson I draw from time lags is the importance of being aware of the relative balances at the individual level. I must not fixate on the much-more-visible group level. Shifts in relative balances at the individual level create and therefore precede changes at the group level. Heat flow peaks at noon; temperature flow peaks in the afternoon.

This reminds me of the three levels with which physicists analyze objects in motion: position, velocity (which is the change in position over time), and acceleration (which is the change in velocity over time). Position and velocity are easy to observe; acceleration is harder. Acceleration, however, is the fundamental level because this is the level at which forces work and initiate change. Position and velocity are consequences of what happens at the level of acceleration. If I want to make changes in position or velocity, I must apply forces to change the acceleration and be prepared to navigate some tricky time lags in the meantime. A ferry boat, for example, must reverse its engines as it approaches the dock in order to arrive at the correct position of the dock with the proper velocity of zero.

I've summarized this lesson to myself with a maxim: *Acceleration, not position*. This advice has reduced the amount of energy I expend worrying about my "position" within my community or about keeping up appearances. Status becomes noisy static. Am I applying myself in the direction of the goals important to me? If so, fine. If not, better get started again. Not only does this shift liberate a lot of my energy, it also liberates others from efforts on my part to perceive them as "lower" than me.

Cycles

~

M Y BABY DAUGHTER SITS ON THE FLOOR. She does not yet know how to crawl. I give her a pile of objects to investigate. She is quietly happy for many minutes and then she cries. I look over and see her sitting at the center of an empty, bare circle. All the things I gave to her lie outside the circle, just beyond her reach. I push them all back to her. Contentment returns. Several minutes later, another cry. Again all the toys lie beyond her reach.

Each time I give her the objects, I can predict with mathematical certainty that they will all eventually end up beyond the circle of her reach. As long as she can reach a toy, it is "in play"; the toy can be dropped and tossed again and again. But the moment the object is tossed out of reach, it becomes "out of play," and she will switch to another object. Eventually, all the objects will be out of reach and the game will be over. She will cry for my energy to move things close to her again so the game can continue.

Flows are similar. Things flow "downhill" until they reach the "bottom," where they stop and become "out of play." Everything within the flow will eventually accumulate at the bottom unless a source of energy comes along and lifts them back "into play." This recycling energy transforms a one-time flow into a repeating cycle. Without this uplifting energy, a flow will eventually pool at the bottom and "die."

In a world several billions of years old, every flow should have reached the bottom by now. This ancient world should be lying still, and yet it is covered with flows. This implies that everything I see flowing over the surface of this ancient Earth is part of a cycle. Any material that flowed to the bottom and couldn't be lifted back into a cycle is still lying down there.

Being lifted back up is very different from flowing down. Flowing "releases" energy and happens spontaneously. Lifting requires energy; it does not happen spontaneously. Every cycle is like a roller coaster that must have a motor to pull the cars from the lowest point (where the ride would otherwise end) to the top of the tallest hill. Each cycle has two parts: the "lifting up" part that requires energy and the "flowing down" part that releases energy. All the changes I see can be thought of as either moving "up" or flowing "down." Blossoming flowers move "up" while rotting leaves and weathering rocks flow "down." A cow pie flows "down" at the same time the grass it nourishes is lifted "up." This dimension of "being lifted up" and "flowing down" gives a new texture to the world I see.

Spring's increasing inflow of sunlight, for example, activates an upward surge of growth from the ground. Each species grows in a different pattern. The stems of bracken ferns unroll from the ground upward. The unrolling stem exposes smaller rolls unrolling into pairs of "leaves," revealing smaller rolls unrolling into pairs of "leaflets." The wave of energy surging up each fern and diffusing outward into every leaflet reminds me of an ocean wave surging into tidepools and diffusing out into every pool and crack.

As energy flows up through winter-dormant branches, buds swell. A wave of leafing out sweeps up the branches. The tips of many branches almost glow with lustrous energy in the spring. By running my gaze from this tip down along the stem, I observe a gradient of increasingly older leaves, which reveals the process by which a bud expands into a leaf over several days. I discover how all the features of the mature leaf exist preformed within the bud. The leaf does not grow so much as it unfolds and expands. The plants of spring are bursting forth like slow-motion fireworks in a swelling celebration of the upward direction.

Energy lifts the earth into expanding green leaves. Yet as I examine the stem's gradient from youngest leaf to oldest, I also see brown spots and holes expanding. The older a leaf, the more holes and brown spots it has. The moment a leaf emerges, it becomes potential food for insects. The gradient of being eaten coexists with the gradient of growth. The "ups" and "downs" of different cycles intertwine.

In spring's increasing flood of sunlight, however, the flow of energy into leaves is far greater than the flow of leaves into animals. The world fills with green leaves, allowing the populations of leaf-eating animals to expand to their annual peaks. They, in turn, provide enough meat for the animal-eating animals to raise their young. Bug-eating birds fill the spring with nesting songs.

However, as daylength decreases through the summer, the uplifting energy subsides. Relative balances begin to shift. Holes in leaves grow faster than leaves. Animal populations begin their decline toward their late-winter lows. Bird songs quiet to chirps and chips. By autumn, dying leaves drop onto the ground, where they decay into minerals that sink deep into the soil until the energy of a future spring lifts them into the sky again.

The Flow of Energy

⟋⟍

I MENTIONED EARLIER how turkey vultures led me to a freshly killed deer just a hundred yards behind my residence. The mountain lion returned that night to eat its fill. When I visited the deer the next morning, blowflies were beginning to swarm upon the remaining carcass. I began visiting the carcass at least twice a day to observe what would happen. I didn't know then how much time I would eventually spend sitting there in the desert or how watching the deer turn into a skeleton would affect my spirit.

The vultures and blowflies arrived first. I'm not sure what the eight to ten vultures did (except that they ate the deer's eyeballs first), because they always flew away as I drew near. But the iridescent blue and green blowflies could be observed from a few inches away. The blowflies did not come to eat the deer. The carcass summoned them to mate and lay eggs within its meat.

In the cool of morning, the bushes for yards around were thick with sluggish flies. As the Sun warmed the air, the flies returned to their carcass orgy. The blowfly population peaked during the second day at what I estimated to be four to five thousand flies. I could hear their buzzing as I approached. Thousands of females laid thousands of eggs. The frantic orgy continued on the deer with no indication of the million tiny maggots hatching from those eggs, burrowing into the safety and nourishment of the meat, and growing beneath the surface.

In a few days, the fly orgy was over. The blowflies departed and never returned—except for an occasional fly that followed the faint whiff of something dead to the scene, found no meat or mate, and flew on. The blowflies must have evolved the collective wisdom not to waste energy laying eggs on something already filled with growing maggots, because the nourishing meat will be eaten or dried up before a late-arriving egg can hatch and reach the "adolescence" of the pupal stage.

Other kinds of flies, however, began to appear on the deer. I tried to keep track by giving them descriptive names. I identified "gray fly" and "brown fly." But when I visited in the afternoon, I found two kinds of brown fly, so the new one became "golden brown fly". The next day, I added "gray fly with black stripes" and "bouncy wing fly." Although I noted many species on the deer, only a few individuals of each species appeared. These flies transacted no frantic business, no hurried orgy, as had occupied the blowflies. I saw some of the species only on the fur, others only on the greasy bones.

Within a few days, the growing mass of maggots (and the diminishing amount of meat) forced the maggots to the surface. The carcass seethed with maggots. There were so many maggots I could hear them wriggling past one another. As the growing maggots transformed the dead deer meat into living maggot meat, the predators moved in. Just as maggots can eat the deer but not the leaves that fed the deer, so there are predators that can eat the maggots but not the deer meat that fed the maggots. One major predator I called "tiger beetle" (the common name is rove beetle) because it was black and pale yellow and ferociously ate maggots in a few gulps.

Other predators hunted other prey. Several species of robber fly sat around the perimeter of the carcass. At unpredictable times, one would buzz across the deer and catch a flying insect in midair. The robber fly landed, sucked its victim's juices, dropped the body, and sat digesting. Parasitic wasps hovered about the scene, injecting their eggs into other insects. The larval wasp will hatch within the victim and feed on and grow within its living body just as the maggots had hatched, fed, and grown within the deer carcass.

By now the stink had subsided. I was down on my hands and knees, eyeball to antennae with this fascinating, increasingly complex community. I lifted a corner of the carcass to see if anything was underneath and discovered large, beautiful orange and black carrion beetles and a multitude of tiny mites. I went out one night and heard a whirring. I turned on my flashlight and saw a large moth licking the bones. Tan beetles with dome-like bodies (troglodyte beetles) lumbered away from the light.

A complex community with a day shift and a night shift had assembled on this deer. Different members of the community worked on different parts of the carcass. What fascinated me about this complicated community was how it all depended on finding a recently dead animal at some unknown point in a vast desert. How did all these different species find their way here in time? Probably many are extremely sensitive to the aroma of death. Do others watch the turkey vultures or listen for the collective whine of blowflies? What were all these insects doing before they found this carcass? How would this community be different if some of the species had not found this carcass? How would this community be different if this deer had died in the nearby mountains?

This complex community, unique to this particular deer, seemed to be based on luck. And yet the many obvious relationships among the species, and the way different species inhabited different parts of the deer at different times, suggested that these ways of life are ancient and well-established. The existence of this community helped me realize that a certain amount of life in an area guarantees a certain amount of death. There will always be a carcass out there somewhere.

⌣

The flowing down of death intertwines with the lifting up of life. The Sun's energy had lifted water and earth into leaves of energy. The deer had broken down those leaves and used their energy to build up its body. The Sun's energy still vibrated within the deer's dead body. The mountain lion, the vultures, and the insects broke down the body and used its energy to sustain themselves and raise the next generation.

This intertwining series of ups and downs reminds me of the roller coaster metaphor that I used in the last chapter. The Sun is the motor that pulls the cars to the top of the first hill. After that initial lift, no other hill requires a motor. The rush down from each summit will carry the cars over the crest of the next hill. Energy's ability to be transformed from downward momentum into upward motion allows a free fall to transform into a much longer and more exciting ride. But the ride cannot last forever.

A fundamental constraint of the universe limits the length of the ride. The next hill cannot be as high as the preceding hill, because not all the energy from the downward plunge will be available for the ascent. Friction, for example, will change some of the careening energy into heat. The cars can never coast up as high as they began. Therefore, each hill must be progressively lower until the cars slow to a stop at the bottom of the ride.

This fundamental constraint (which is part of the Second Law of Thermodynamics) shapes the transformations of energy within this dead deer. Not all the energy the maggots harvest from the deer can become maggot bodies. Some of the energy will be spent in wriggling and feeding and defecation. So a hundred pounds of deer meat will create far less than a hundred pounds of maggots. A pound of maggots will feed only a few ounces of rove beetles. Similarly, a deer must eat far more than its body weight of leaves and a mountain lion must eat many deer over the course of its life. The "inefficiency" of these energy transfers sets limits. The desert can support only so many deer; a deer herd can support only so many mountain lions; the deer carcass can support only so many insects. As the deer's energy is passed on, the community sustained by that energy must dwindle and eventually come to an end.

One day, the surviving maggots began to drop out of the body and wriggle across the ground. A foot or so away, they burrowed into the ground, where they would enter the dormant pupal stage. They had consumed enough energy to complete the transformation into sexually mature adult blowflies, but that metamorphosis would take time. The carcass, crawling with predators, was too dangerous a place. Since the maggots had gathered all they needed from the deer, they left it and burrowed down to a safer place where they could survive the inactive period of metamorphosis. As the maggots departed, many of the other insects did too. Within a few hours, all the "big black beetles" crawled off the deer, climbed up nearby stalks of grass and flew heavily away. I was sad to see them go. Our community was breaking up.

After the maggots left, a few new species moved in. Most prominent were the bone-cleaning dermestid beetles and the small "green shiny beetles." Only a hundred or so individuals lived on the carcass now. All that was left was hide, bits of dried meat, cartilage, and bone. A quietness settled in. Change was slow. In the beginning, the carcass had changed quickly. Ten or fifteen new species might arrive each day. But now each day was pretty much like any other. A spider spun her web within the dried leather skin to catch any insect passing by. There wasn't much energy left here. I visited less, watched the desert more, and grew philosophical.

This is how the roller coaster ride coasts to an end. The energy within the deer had nourished more than 130 species over several weeks. The minerals within its body are now within other creatures. Those creatures will find other carrion, reproduce, and carry on. The minerals will keep cycling through bodies, soil, and plants for millions of years. But not so with the energy in the deer. It has flowed away.

Energy flows "down" in the sense that it loses the ability to do work. This is not because there is less energy. The amount of energy remains the same—a fact scientists label the First Law of Thermodynamics—just as the amount of water remains the same as it flows downhill. What decreases is the energy's ability to do work. Energy becomes "old and tired," less concentrated, and less available for work. When I heard the maggots wriggling past one another, for example, that was some of the energy within the deer's body becoming sound energy, a vibration of air molecules. The energy within that wriggling sound is still with us many years later but it is so diffused among an uncountable vastness of air molecules that the energy is unrecoverable, unusable ever again.

Scientists define the direction of energy's flow in terms of "entropy," a mathematical concept not easy to describe. I will use a more lyrical image, that of flowing "down" toward fewer possibilities. Energy makes things possible, but as it flows "down," the same amount of energy can no longer do as much. Less becomes possible. Therefore, the direction of energy's overall flow is toward fewer possibilities—a fact scientists label the Second Law of Thermodynamics.

Individual fragments of energy can be lifted up toward more possibilities, just as individual water droplets can splash upward within a cascade. However, each upward splash is only possible because a far greater amount of water plunges down the cascade. In the very same way, each upward rush of a roller coaster is only possible because of the greater plunge that preceded it. Energy can be lifted up but only if a greater amount flows down somewhere else.

Every living thing needs energy. We need energy to breathe, move, make sound, eat, grow, think, repair our bodies. But with every sound, move, and breath we make, energy flows away from us. This creates a pattern of energy harvesting that I see throughout the world.

The only way to remain balanced within the relentless outflow is to harvest energy from elsewhere. The deer harvests the leaves. The mountain lion harvests the deer. The maggots harvest the remainder of the deer. The rove beetles harvest the maggots. (Harvesting does not necessarily mean eating. A cat sleeping in a warm patch of sunlight harvests solar energy. We harvest energy when we gather firewood.)

The same pattern of harvesting energy from the greater system can be found on smaller levels, too. Within the animals, each cell harvests energy from the energy-laden blood streaming by. The only way the bloodstream can maintain this richness is by harvesting energy from the digestive system. The only way the digestive system can maintain itself within the relentless harvesting of the bloodstream is by harvesting energy from plants or meat. Everywhere, energy is flowing "down" and everywhere, on all scales, living systems are maneuvering so that some of the energy within the greater system flows through them.

The community on the dead deer is dependent on the energy within the deer in the same way we are dependent on the energy from the Sun. I watch an active, complex living community dwindling to a quiet skeleton and I think, "This is how the world will end." When the Sun runs down, life will cease, the Earth's cycles will flow down and stop, and the world will become still.

I look out over the desert, out over this lovely, lovely world. I don't want this ride to end. I long to help it last longer, but what can I do? The Second Law of Thermodynamics shapes everything I do. It constrains me in the same way it constrains the roller coaster; any upward movement can happen only if there is a greater downward movement elsewhere. I can create possibilities only by using up more possibilities. Anything I do to make the ride last longer only makes it end sooner. The Second Law of Thermodynamics drags down my spirit's upward aspirations. I despair at not being able to do more than live at the expense of the world. The rotting deer gave form to this despair, creating a bittersweet burden I carried for many years. Part of the story I tell in the next part of the book is how a spiral of visions and actions released me from this burden.

⌒

The deer died in early September. I left the area in early January. Before I left, I went out for one last sit. I had not visited the place for a month. The hide and most of the bones were gone, probably carried away by coyotes. Memories of flies swarming in the summer heat felt very distant from the few bleached bones lying quietly in the winter cold.

I picked up a leg bone and hit it against a rock. The bone split open and there within its marrow were "green shiny beetles." The energy ride from the deer was not over yet. The ride was down to a few individuals of one species, but the ride of intertwining ups and downs had not yet reached its bottom.

Shifting Balances

Two Canyons

I LED TOURS OF CLIFF DWELLINGS for three summers. The two largest abandoned villages lay in two different canyons. To reach the ruins in Aspen Canyon, we followed a trail that switch-backed down a steep, rocky cliff to the canyon floor. There we entered a magic forest of aspens, Douglas fir, and oak trees. Dogwoods and sweet peas grew in the cool shade. Breezes rustled through the leaves overhead while lizards scuttled through the carpet of fallen leaves below. Birds sang throughout the forest. I could look up through quivering green leaves and see canyon walls rising into the clear blue summer sky. Grumbling and nagging gave way to audible sighs of relaxation when the people on the tour reached the canyon bottom. Softness returned to each step. This forest, with its green light and cool shade, with its bird songs and plant oxygen, always had a calming, healing effect on people.

Walking within Sand Canyon was a different experience. No aspens grew in Sand Canyon. A few scrub oaks grew against the canyon walls, but the canyon floor was covered with sagebrush, cheat grass, and soft sand. Prickly seeds of cheat grass filled socks and itched ankles. Feet slipped in loose sand. Unshaded, sandy ground reflected the Sun's heat. Sand Canyon strolls were postponed until the cool of evening or early morning.

The puzzling difference between the two canyons is the stream. A year-round stream flows the entire length of Sand Canyon, while Aspen Canyon has no stream. Aspen Canyon does have a streambed, but water flows along it only during a heavy storm. A paradox! A stream flows in the desert canyon; no water flows in the forested canyon. This does not fit. It should be the other way around. What is happening here?

I learned through reading that Sand Canyon had not always been so barren. In the late 1800s, the first white explorers described Sand Canyon as choked with scrub oak. They reported ponds and marshes, ducks and geese. Observation cards from the 1910s and 1920s recorded birds in the canyon that have not been seen since. Only recently has Sand Canyon become a sandy canyon of sagebrush. How did this happen?

More than fifty years ago, massive overgrazing (first by sheep, later by cattle) began a process of erosion called arroyo-cutting. *Arroyo* is the Spanish word for the steep-walled, unvegetated gullies that are all too common in the arid Southwest. Sand Canyon's stream flows at the bottom of an arroyo so deep that I had assumed it to be an inner canyon thousands of years old. The walls of this "inner canyon" rise fifty feet above the stream and then level into flat sandy terraces that extend to the base of the cliffs.

These sandy terraces mark where the oak-choked canyon floor had been. Sand, fifty feet deep throughout the entire canyon system, had once formed a level canyon floor. This former canyon bottom had been fifty feet above the present arroyo bottom. The level, sandy terraces are all that remain of this former bottom. Yet how could the appearance of the arroyo influence the vegetation within the canyon?

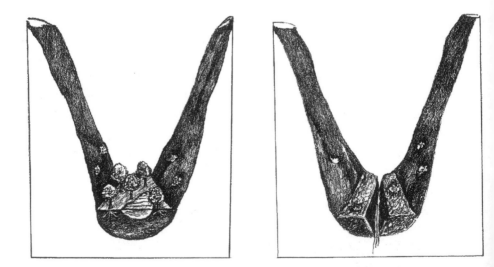

Sand Canyon was once a place of oaks and marshes. Now an arroyo deeply dissects sandy terraces.

The region averages only eleven inches of precipitation per year. However, the canyons are surrounded by bare sandstone mesas. Snowmelt and rain flow easily across those slickrock surfaces, converge into streams, and cascade over the cliffs into the canyons. Once in the canyon, this concentration of water sinks into fifty feet of porous sand. Its speed slows to a few percolating feet per hour.

A hundred years ago, this water had to percolate through sand the entire length of the canyon—many miles. The sandy canyon bottom slowed the outflow of water so dramatically that outflow was much less than the annual inflow of runoff from the surrounding mesas. Groundwater accumulated within the sand. The water table rose. Even though no water flowed on the surface, abundant water slowly percolated beneath the surface. The scrub oaks of Sand Canyon sent their roots into this reservoir of water. In some places, the water table did rise to the surface, forming marshes and ponds for waterfowl.

⌒

But when the arroyo sliced down through the fifty feet of sand, it created a new path for groundwater. Instead of percolating through sand the entire length of the canyon (a route that took years), the groundwater could now percolate a hundred feet to the arroyo in the middle of the canyon. There it emerged as seeps and springs. Once at the surface, the water became free to flow several miles per hour as a stream. Water that once took several years to leave the canyon now flows away in several hours. This drastic acceleration of outflow shifted the relative balance.

Water flowed away faster than it entered and the amount of groundwater diminished. The water table dropped farther beneath the surface, out of reach of the oaks. They died and their bare gray trunks eventually fell. The deeper the arroyo, the farther the groundwater dropped below the level of the terraces. Only plants that can survive with eleven inches of direct precipitation now grow on the terraces. A canyon bottom of trees became remnant terraces of sagebrush and cheat grass perched above the arroyo. The canyon lies gashed with gullies, its life water oozing away. Sand Canyon is withering precisely because of the stream running its entire length.

The cliff dwellings are sheltered from the rain, so the ancient buildings remain dry and well-preserved. The original wood remains solid and

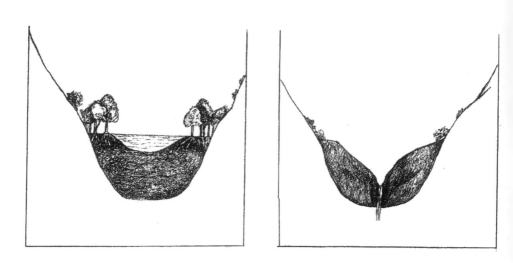

The arroyo creates a quick exit for the groundwater, draining the canyon of possibilities.

identifiable. Most of the wood used in Aspen Canyon's town is aspen. That makes sense, because the town looks out on a canyon filled with aspen. However, most of the wood used in Sand Canyon's town is also aspen. This suggests that aspens were growing in Sand Canyon when the town builders came seven hundred years ago. Sand Canyon then looked like Aspen Canyon today. Yet the aspens were not there when our culture arrived six hundred years later. What happened to the aspens?

Archaeological remains suggest that these people once lived and farmed many miles farther downstream. Because of a drought and/or because of their farming practices, erosion began. Geological evidence reveals another arroyo forming in this area seven hundred years ago. As the arroyo grew, harvests dwindled. Some of the people moved upstream of the arroyo and built the cliff dwellings we tour today.

Once an arroyo begins, however, it can easily continue to cut its way headward. The arroyo slowly followed those people upcanyon, creeping around each curve in the canyon until even the old people in the town could look out and see the arroyo gnawing its way around the final bend and consuming their fields.

What did those people think as they watched trees reluctantly topple into the widening gully? What did they feel as they watched side gullies gradually dissect the beautiful canyon bottom into isolated terraces? Did they ask why the powers of the world were withering this green canyon? Did they wonder whether they had done something wrong to offend those powers? Did they discuss what they should do differently next time?

Corn could be grown only by carrying pot after pot of water up the steep, sandy bank of the deepening arroyo. An easy life became harder and harder. Since the head of this box canyon was only two miles away, the people could not move upcanyon again. Soon they would have to leave the canyon system that had been home for many generations. Where would they go?

Archaeologists say the cliff dwellers lived here only fifteen to thirty years. After they left, the canyon healed. Over the centuries, the arroyo filled in, the water table rose, and oak trees recolonized the canyon. Aspens did not return. Perhaps they would have returned eventually, but too many sheep were brought into the area about fifty years ago and this second arroyo began to grow.

The canyon now erodes around me just as it eroded around the earlier dwellers of this canyon. When I see the edge of a terrace crumble and slide into the stream or when I see a dying tree leaning toward the arroyo, I see the same things those ancient people saw as they watched their hopes slip and flow away.

First Visions of Gaia

$\smile$

FTER SPENDING TWO YEARS in the canyons, I
read *Gaia: A New Look at Life*, by James Lovelock. In his
book, Lovelock points out that many "unchanging" characteristics of the
Earth's atmosphere are actually unstable. Oxygen, for example, makes up
twenty-one percent of our atmosphere, and yet atmospheric oxygen is
explosively unstable. Whenever there is a fire, whether it be a match, an
explosion in the cylinder of an internal combustion engine, or a forest
fire, oxygen is leaving the atmosphere to combine with the material that
is burning. Oxygen combines with blood hemoglobin at every breath.
Oxygen combines with iron to form rust. If left to itself, oxygen will
combine with other molecules and disappear from the atmosphere as it
did on rusty red Mars. The fact that our atmosphere has remained
twenty-one percent oxygen over many millennia means that there must
be a flow of oxygen into the atmosphere large enough to balance the
rapid outflow. Plants produce this enormous flow. They exhale enough
oxygen to "bury" us beneath miles of it.

Lovelock also points out that, although great geological changes have
occurred since life first flourished, conditions on the Earth's surface have
remained remarkably constant at levels close to those optimal for life.
This led Lovelock and Lynn Margulis to their hypothesis that life, in a
collective sense, has evolved the ability to create and maintain an environment favorable for life. This global regulation works almost as if all
life on the planet were part of one global living thing. Lovelock refers to
the Earth as Gaia whenever he wants to emphasize life's influence on the
planet. This name (from the Greek goddess of Earth) suggests a weaving
together of our concepts of life and Earth into something greater. The

name is mythic but the hypothesis is scientific throughout and is still being debated.

Lovelock's book altered the assumptions with which I looked at the world. The rest of this book describes the consequences of that change. If you enjoy the rest of this book, you will enjoy Lovelock's book. However, if my conclusions seem unscientific or fallacious to you, please do not generalize your opinion to the scientific Gaia Hypothesis. Please consider that on its own merits.

⌒

Shortly after I read Lovelock's book, a friend and I went camping in the autumn. We pitched our tent above timberline and went for an afternoon walk. Since we planned to hike for only a few hours, we set off with no supplies. We rounded a summit and came upon a spectacular ridge connecting two mountains. The farther mountain looked like a magnificent climb; we set off toward it. Walking that tundra ridge was a celebration. The wind blew bracing and chill, invigorating us as we walked along the sinuous gentle pathway two miles high.

The mountain was bigger and farther than we had realized. We walked faster, partly to try to get to the mountain and back before dark and partly to stay warm. The Sun had moved behind clouds in the west and the wind was now strong and cold.

We could feel how stressful the wind must be for the few plants growing on the ridge. The wind blows away any heat the plants gather from the Sun and sucks away valuable moisture. The wind abrades the plants with sand in the summer and sharp ice crystals in the winter. Plants can survive up here only if they can get out of the wind, so the plants grow low to the ground in the shelter of rocks. Patches of life extend downwind from the rocks like shadows. The windshelter of each rock extends only so far. Taller rocks have longer plant shadows. Examples of this Fit between wind-sheltering rocks and plants covered the ridge.

The Earth's shadow rose into the sky and we were far from camp. The mountain still loomed in the distance. We turned back. The day's heat had been blown away and now the growing chill of evening was gusting past us. I had a warm wind breaker, but my friend had only a sweater, which the wind easily pierced. The Fit between rocks and plants inspired me to walk on her upwind side and block the wind for her.

Walking within my wind shadow kept her from growing quite so cold.

We heard a sound overhead and saw a V-shaped flock of geese approaching the ridge. The flock came on slowly because it was flying straight into the mountain wind. As the wedge of geese passed low overhead, I noticed that the leaders kept exchanging places several times each minute. The lead goose is like a ridge rock; it cleaves the wind and creates a windshelter behind it. Yet no single goose has the strength to lead indefinitely. By dropping back into the shelter of the flock, a goose could regather the strength needed to lead the flock again against the wind. Trading places allowed the flock to fly with greater strength.

The geese suggested a way we could stay warm as we hurried back toward camp. When my friend grew cold, I took off my windbreaker, gave it to her, and walked in her windshadow. The shelter of the jacket allowed her to regain her warmth. Without my jacket, I began to grow cold, though walking in her shelter kept me from cooling as quickly as I otherwise would have. When I began to shiver, we traded the jacket. In its shelter, I regained my warmth, while my friend started to cool down. When she became chilled, we traded again. Back and forth we traded the jacket as we returned along the darkening ridge. In this way, we both maintained a temperature somewhere between the warmth of the jacket and the cold of the cutting wind. We returned to our tent in the starlight, exhilarated.

The cold wind and starlit ridge were physically exhilarating. Yet there was more to the exhilaration than that. A magically luminous new image of the world was growing within me. Helping one another along that ridge and experiencing how one life can make possible another life had given me a key to understanding Gaia. That dark, windswept walk and the wedge of geese cleaving the wind formed my first visions of Gaia.

Second Visions of Gaia

~~

A FEW WEEKS LATER, my mind still sparkling from that walk, I went hiking into the Rockies, high up into the granite basins that cradled glaciers during the Ice Age. The flowing glaciers scraped and smoothed the bedrock of these basins. When the glaciers melted away several thousand years ago, they left behind polished granite, bare and lifeless. Life is recolonizing the basins, but at this high elevation the growing season is short. Growth is slow. Much of the area remains bare granite. The calls of a passing flock of rosy finches are heard within the stillness. In this land of white snowbanks and gray rock, emerald green mats of moss catch the eye.

I gazed at the contrast between the gray granite, bare except for occasional splotches of lichens, and a thick mat of green moss. This contrast led me to focus more precisely on the edge between them. The edge of the mat was not moss but a thin, dry, pale green crust. A lichen splotch protruded from beneath the pale green crust. I peeled back the pale green crust and saw the rest of the lichen splotch buried and rotting into brown "soil." Oh, now I understand! The lichen had been there first, but it was being covered by the crust. This led me to notice that the pale green crust was, in turn, being covered by the moss. The mat was expanding. The crust was the front line of advancement with the moss following after.

Grasses and flowers grew near the center of the mat. For some reason, they did not grow near the edge. As I crawled toward them my knees and hands grew damp. The center of the mat was a thick, squishy sponge. I probed into the spongy surface near the center and found a brownish "soil" containing the dead, decaying bodies of previous

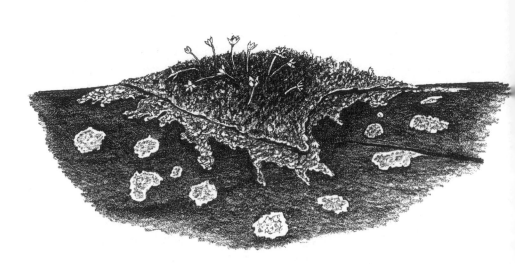

Life expands over bedrock through a spiral of change. Each expansion of life creates conditions for a further expansion of life.

generations of plants mixed with sand and dust. When I had flecked away the dry crust on the edge, bedrock had been right beneath. The edge of the mat is thinner than the center because the edge is younger and has not been there as long.

This gradient from thin edge to thick center, from dry bedrock to damp soil, from pale green crust to flowers reveals the spiral of change by which life expands over bare rock. The sponge-like structure of moss absorbs the melting snow. This moisture allows the moss to grow even after the bedrock around it becomes stone-dry. Any dust blown across the mat of moss drops into the moss, out of the wind. The mat accumulates dust just as flypaper accumulates flies. The moistened dust and the rotting plants of earlier generations release nutrients that nourish the next generation of moss growing above. With each generation, the clump builds upon itself and creates a deeper, more nourishing soil beneath. As the mat expands in size, it absorbs more snowmelt. The moist mat grows thick and fertile enough to support flowering plants. Grasses grow taller than the moss, extending the clump's wind-baffling ability upward and trapping more dust. Flowers attract insects. As these insects defecate, lay eggs, and die, they introduce new chemicals that nourish new possibilities. Flowering plants produce seeds that attract birds which drop other fertilizing chemicals upon the growing clump. The mat grows thicker and more diverse with time.

The accumulating dust weights the clump in place. Roots from new plants search out tiny cracks in the bedrock and root the clump to the mountain. The securely anchored clump can now "ooze" over edges and spread down steeper slopes just as rock climbers can rappel down cliffs once their ropes are secured to well-anchored points. The mat of moss expands from a secure center onto slopes that otherwise would be too steep for colonization.

In this land of steep bedrock, the influence of gravity is stronger than lowlanders may have experienced. A dislodged rock bounds down the granite slopes and gathers momentum at a frightening rate. The faster it goes, the more crazily it ricochets off the slope, until it either reaches the bottom hundreds of feet below or smashes against bedrock with such force that it shatters into rock shrapnel.

While scrambling up a steep slope, I dislodged a large rock. I turned to watch it bound away. It began to tumble down the steep, moss-covered slope. Each time the rock bounced upon the mat of moss, the moss absorbed much of the rock's impact. The rock squished to a surprisingly quick stop after three or four bounces.

The rock lay on top of the moss. Around it lay other rocks at various stages of being engulfed by growing moss. These rocks do not tip when I step on them. These rocks will not tumble again. The mats are like spider webs, trapping the rocks that pass by and absorbing them into the growing web.

Mats of moss also stretch across channels of meltwater. The water must flow over and through the moss. Rock particles swept along by the water are quickly filtered out. The trapped rocks thicken the filter of moss, helping it trap even more rocks.

Mats of moss slow the outflow of rocks from the mountains. They shift the relative balance so that more of the weathering rock accumulates high in the basin rather than flowing down to the river valleys far below. The gravity-powered conveyor belt backs up. Growing moss mats and trapped rocks bury the polished granite.

Water is a scarce resource on bare bedrock. Once snow melts from a slope, the non-absorbent granite becomes stone-dry and hostile to life. But a moss sponge can absorb water from a channel and spread it throughout the sponge, allowing plants to grow far away from the streams. During the hot days of August, the moss absorbs meltwater from snowbanks higher on the mountain. Drought won't cut the summer growing season short.

Before life expanded in this basin, no mats of moss grew to absorb that snowmelt. All the trickles of meltwater converged into streams that raced down the polished bedrock to the valley below. The entire drainage flowed with more volume, speed, and power. The river in the valley below was a powerful torrent.

However, over thousands of years, more of the trickles were intercepted by the expanding moss and spread over the slope. This spread out moisture evaporates as it warms on the sunny slopes. Snowmelt that would otherwise flow down out of the basin as liquid now rises up as vapor. The mats divert snowmelt away from the streams, back into the sky whence the snow fell. The mats of moss are altering the outflow of water from this basin just as they are altering the outflow of rocks.

As I hiked down out of the basin, I noticed other ways that life diverts water away from its seaward flow. Beavers create ponds that slow the streams. A deer drinks from a stream and bounds away carrying a bit of the stream uphill. The deer will breathe some of that stream into the air and urinate some upon the soil. Insects emerging from the water carry molecules of water within them. The amount of moisture within a mosquito is tiny, but sometimes there are billions of mosquitoes! Cottonwoods and willows root in the moist riverbank and exhale enormous amounts of water vapor into the air. Even the water that flows on to the sea does not escape life's influence. This water must flow slower because the speed of flowing water depends on its volume. When life reduces the volume of water flowing within a channel, the remaining water must flow more slowly.

When I was a child, I was taught a very simple version of the water cycle. I learned that water evaporates from the ocean, falls on the land as snow or rain, and then flows back to the ocean again. But the cycle is not that simple. As water flows back toward the ocean, it can be detoured onto a million paths that lead it to evaporate, form clouds, and fall as rain again.

Back home among books, I learned that only 11 inches of the land's annual precipitation comes directly from the ocean. If the water did cycle in the simple way I learned in school, the land would receive only 11 inches of precipitation per year, barely enough moisture to support arid grasslands. However, as this moisture flows back toward the sea, some of it evaporates and falls again as rain upon the land. And some of that recycled rainfall evaporates and falls again and yet again. Each time the water falls, it can nourish life. As a result of this recycling, an average of 29 inches of moisture falls onto the land each year. The recycling of fresh water back into the sky expands the ocean's gift of 11 inches to a total of 29 inches, enough moisture to support forests.

Before plants colonized land 450 million years ago, the land was bare rock. No absorbent soil existed, because soil is a product of life. Rain falling on a rocky, pre-life world would have run off much faster than it does today. More of the rain would have flowed straight back to the sea. Only scattered puddles and damp rock surfaces would be left to evaporate in the sunlight and be recycled. Less recycling meant less rain would fall.

But then plants spread over the land and began to absorb the rain. Through a spiral of change, plants recycled more rain and more rain nourished more life until forests and prairies covered much of the Earth. Observing mats of moss expand within that glaciated basin was like watching primitive algae and mosses colonize the rocky continents 450 million years ago. Mats of moss spreading over granite gave me my second vision of Gaia as a great spiral of change by which life transformed a rocky world into the green Earth we know today.

Within the Wedge of Life

I WAS HIKING ACROSS the steep slopes of a desert ridge. The ridge was composed of loose rocks that normally slide underfoot. Yet, this year, the slopes felt firm. A dislodged rock did not tumble or dislodge other rocks. The previous year had been much wetter than normal and an abundance of vining plants had covered these slopes. Their stems had now dried into thin but surprisingly strong, desert-gray cords. Life had used the gift of abundant rain to create a bizarre net that would hold these loose slopes together and slow erosion for some time to come.

The dead trees that fell into the large mountain lake over the years have floated to its outlet, where they have accumulated because the outlet is too narrow for logs to pass through. Water flowing out of the lake must flow through the cracks and gaps between these logs. The water can flow through, but sticks get stuck in the gaps. This narrows the gaps enough for twigs to get stuck. They narrow the gaps enough for pine needles, seeds, and insect bodies to get stuck. The log jam strains out floating things, which help form a dam oozing water its entire length.

This dam detains many acre-feet of the spring melt-off. If not detained, this water would have converged with the melt-off of other streams, swelling the erosive power downstream. The log-jam dam reduces erosion by buffering the daily and seasonal pulse of melt-off. After the surge of melt-off subsides, the water detained by the dam oozes through and the dam dries out.

While examining the dried-out dam, I realized that all the floating things it had strained out were creations of life. Before life appeared on this planet, the only things that floated were ice and some airy lavas. Now, things that float are so common that I take them for granted, not realizing how unusual is each floating leaf, twig, and seed.

⌐⌐

I was thinking about mats of moss covering smooth, glacial bedrock as I walked through a forest. How did this forested place look before life? Without life, this forest would be just a bare bedrock surface. Within the forest, I suddenly became aware of life as a creator of surfaces. Trees tower a hundred feet into the air, branching intricately into smaller and smaller twigs with each twig sending out a multitude of broad-surfaced leaves. Each trunk has a richly furrowed bark whose creases and ridges provide a wealth of nooks and crannies within which tiny insects lay eggs, spiders spin webs, and birds probe with their beaks.

Beneath the trees lie the abundant surfaces of fallen leaves decaying into soil that is filled with roots branching into a multitude of rootlets and root hairs. Each rootlet provides a juicy surface upon which some tiny insect might suck. Roots worm between soil fragments in search of moisture soupy rich in dissolved minerals. The roots probe downward until they creep across bedrock, searching for cracks to explore. The roots pry open cracks and split bedrock, creating still more surfaces deep beneath the ground.

Every animal in this forest is filled with abundant surfaces because the biological processes of life depend on surfaces. The convoluted structure of lungs creates a huge surface where circulating blood can absorb the inhaled oxygen. The looped structure of intestines creates an enormous surface where circulating blood can absorb the digested food. Capillaries create a vast network of surfaces where the blood, now rich with oxygen and food, can contact and nourish the billions of cells within a body. Feathers and fur, full of air-trapping surfaces, surround and insulate warm-blooded birds and mammals. By increasing surfaces, life alters the rates of the chemical and physical reactions occurring on these surfaces.

Bare bedrock possesses a minimum of surface. The process by which plants transform bedrock into forest is called succession. I had always thought of this process as a competitive surge upward for the limited resource of sunlight in which the losers were shaded out. But now I begin to think of succession as life's sunlight-fueled creation of surfaces, one of the most limited resources of all. Life creates surfaces because life needs surfaces. Life photosynthesizes along surfaces, breathes and digests along surfaces, sits on surfaces, sleeps on surfaces, lays eggs on surfaces. Life has created so many surfaces that reactions now happen at immense rates that were impossible when the Earth was simple bedrock.

Thinking of surfaces deepens my understanding of photosynthesis. I had always thought of photosynthesis as the process by which plants convert sunlight into chemical energy. But it is more than an energy conversion. Photosynthesis is the process by which plants, using solar energy, convert carbon dioxide (CO_2) and water (H_2O) into sugar ($C_6H_{12}O_6$) and atmospheric oxygen (O_2), which is vented into the atmosphere and gratefully taken in by lungs, gills, spiracles, and stomata throughout the world. A different way to think of this is that photosynthesis is the magic process by which life combines two formless things (a gas and a liquid) and creates a solid (a molecule of sugar).

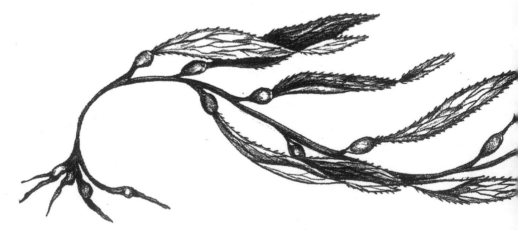

Like a spider, life spins material into amazing, flow-altering structures such as kelp.

All the examples I come upon (the desert vines, things that float, surfaces) are solid structures that were created from air and water and sunlight. In terms of flows, this is one of the most miraculous of all. I look around and see cattail marshes, forests, prairies; all that "stuff" of life was once flowing water, "insubstantial" air and sunlight. So photosynthesis is much more than the transformation of solar energy into chemical energy. It is also the shaping of the formless into form. Each summer day, each acre can produce hundreds of pounds of solid material. The amount is impressive, but even more impressive is the form this material takes. Just as a spider creates a large web from a tiny drop of silk, so life has spun amazing structures originating from the solid sugar molecules of photosynthesis. Over and over, it is the intricate structures and the amazing flow-altering powers within them that transport me with awe.

Along the coast of the Pacific Ocean, extensive kelp beds float out beyond the surf. Kelp, a member of the algae family that helped colonize the ancient Earth, is anchored to the ocean floor, but gas-filled bulbs lift the growing stalks toward the surface. Like barrage balloons floating

into the sky the growing kelp floats up into the waves far above. It is easy to see the effect the ocean has on the kelp when I watch the kelp sway passively back and forth with every wave. It is harder to notice the effect the kelp has on each wave. The kelp forests are deep and very thick. The kelp's calm swaying extracts energy from each wave because the wave is forced to move many tons of kelp. The wave energy that moves kelp is energy that will not reach the shore and pound against our continental foundations. Energy that would otherwise lift and clunk boulders against bedrock instead pushes pliant but heavy kelp fronds harmlessly back and forth. Waves that would pulverize barnacles are diminished to waves that bring food and oxygen to the animals living on the kelp-sheltered tidal rocks. Only after the great storms, when the beaches are covered with kelp ripped from the ocean floor, do I realize the stress the kelp undergoes as it absorbs and dampens the energy within each wave.

All land is part of the cycle of rock being raised above the sea and eroding back down. The relative balance between uplift and erosion determines how much land there is. Ever since oceans existed, the energy of winds has driven waves across the ocean's surface. For billions of years, waves have gnawed at coastlines. Every emerging island or continent must rise through that zone of intense wave erosion, but life has not always been there to intervene between waves and land. I can imagine a time of unhampered waves smashing with full force against the naked bedrock. The land would have fallen back into the sea faster in those pre-kelp, pre-coral times. By reducing wave erosion, life reduces the flow of land back to the ocean. This shifts the relative balance between emergence and erosion, allowing more land to accumulate. Even the continents beneath us are partly a creation of life.

Margulis and Lovelock's Gaia Hypothesis complements and completes Darwin's theory of evolution. Darwin saw how the environment shaped life. Margulis and Lovelock see how life shapes its environment. Together, these two insights reveal a creative interaction between life and its environment. Life and its environment form a spiral of change containing a potential we don't yet understand. The history of evolution is the story of the spiral by which the impossible became possible.

Once upon a time, ultraviolet radiation scoured the Earth with such intensity that life on land was impossible. Life could exist only beneath the radiation barrier of water. The plants that survived within that shelter produced oxygen, some of which diffused into the atmosphere above. As atmospheric oxygen increased, a layer of ozone began to form high in the atmosphere. This layer filtered out some of the radiation. Life no longer needed quite as much water overhead. The underwater shelter expanded closer to the surface. More plants could grow within it and produce more oxygen, which increased the ozone layer, which reduced the ultraviolet radiation, which allowed life to move yet closer to the water's surface. This spiral of change eventually made life on land possible.

Once upon a time, flowers did not exist. Before then, plants had to produce large quantities of pollen to ensure that a few grains of the wind-blown pollen would land on the female part of other individuals of that species. Then insects appeared. Insects could carry grains of pollen against the wind. Insects could be guided by colors, scents, and tastes to deposit pollen precisely upon another flower of the same species. For the plants, it was as if the capricious wind had acquired consciousness. Not as much energy had to go into pollen production. Energy could flow into petals, perfumes, and nectars to lure insects. Insects joined with flowers in a great spiral of change that created the botanical spectacle around us.

Once upon a time, rivers were a one-way flow from the land to the sea. But now they are two-way roads for the salmon that connect the deep ocean with the shallow forest streams where the salmon hatch. The tiny hatchlings follow the rivers down to the sea. There they range far for food, gathering the ocean's fertility into their growing bodies. After three to four years, the salmon return to their rivers with massive bodies powerful enough to swim upstream. Swimming against the current all the way back to their birthplaces is tremendous work; the salmon arrive battered and exhausted. They lay and fertilize their eggs and then die. Their bodies drift downstream. Bears, eagles, and gulls flock to this salmon feast. The fish-stuffed animals defecate abundantly; thousands of tons of nitrogen- and phosphate-rich fertilizer rain upon the forests. It is no coincidence that salmon spawn in areas surrounded by fertile forests; these forests have been receiving a lavish gift of potent fertilizer from the distant sea for millions of years. This upstream-moving gift was impossible a billion years ago. Now it exists.

Once upon a time, sex, vision, flight, and consciousness were impossible. Impossible in the sense that they had never occurred in the entire history of the Earth. But tiny changes kept accumulating and eventually each of them became possible. Life pushes against its edges just as a mat of moss pushes across bedrock. Each expansion creates opportunities for new expressions of life and each new life creates opportunities for further expansion. This spiral of change with all it has made possible and with all it will make possible is what I've come to call Gaia. This spiral created the soft, moist, green world and made possible my ability to be conscious of this miracle. I feel humble gratitude for the life preceding me and the life surrounding me.

‿‿

I remember the wedge of geese flying against the mountain wind. The older members used their mature strength to cleave a passage for the younger members who followed. As the younger geese mature, they shall move forward to help cleave a passage for the next generation.

I envision Gaia as a great wedge of life. The early, primitive bacteria and algae cleaved a passage through the blasting resistance of a harsh, primal environment. Behind them, other life followed. The wedge has now stretched over thousands of millions of years and broadened into millions of species. We humans are part of the recently emerged, youngest generation flying at the very back of the wedge. We fly within the protection of all that has gone before, a protection so vast and powerful that we scarcely feel the harsh resistance of that primal environment.

Gaia's story is not finished. The wedge of life can continue to expand for hundreds of millions of years. As I mature, a desire grows within me to press forward and feel the resisting wind against my face, to help cleave a passage for the impossibilities that can follow.

The Invitation of Gaia

⟋⟍

WHEN I RETURNED TO THE TWO CANYONS, I saw them with new vision. I noticed that when flash floods cascade over the cliffs and flow down through the canyons, the water encounters fallen tree trunks lying across Aspen Canyon's streambed. The surge of water has to stop and fill in behind each dam before it can continue on its way. The fallen trees create a series of broad, flat pools that slow the torrent. Less soil is washed away; more water remains behind. The fallen trees help the next generation of trees.

When summer thunderstorms hurl rain and hail at twenty miles per hour against the ground, that pounding power never reaches the soil of Aspen Canyon. Hail plunging through the upper canopy of aspen branches tears their leaves into tatters, but the leaves reduce the hail's momentum. The hail bounces off the dogwood leaves and drops onto fallen leaves. There it melts and gently percolates through the layer of moldering leaves, dissolving minerals and carrying them into the sandy soil. The plants protect the soil from the hail and the soil absorbs the moisture the plants will need.

This soil will stay fertile as long as it remains warm and moist. The trees form an insulating blanket each night. I was always amazed at how pleasantly warm were the aspen woods when I walked beneath them in the cool midnight moonlight. The trees also gentle the desert Sun with dappled shade. The soil remains warm both night and day instead of alternating between cold and hot. The plants and their mulch also protect the soil's precious moisture from the drying touch of Sun and wind. Any moisture that evaporates from this canyon will pass through leaves in the service of life.

I led a tour to Aspen Canyon in the midst of a horrible sandstorm. Dust blew in our eyes. We covered our noses and mouths with handkerchiefs. But when we reached the woods, we found sanctuary beneath the aspen trees. We heard the wind roaring in the treetops, but the wind could not penetrate the grove of trees. We could breathe easily. The trees slowed the wind; the wind-blown sand dropped to the woodland floor. The trees were gathering more soil for their roots to explore.

Newton said that for every action there is an opposite and equal reaction. When wind buffets a tree, one easily sees the wind's effect upon the tree. But the opposite and equal reaction of the tree's effect upon the wind is harder to see. The wind-tossed tree continually absorbs the wind's energy.

By absorbing the blasting wind, the pounding rain, and the searing Sun, the trees tame great energies. This ability to absorb energy, however, is easily overlooked. I remain unaware of how much energy is being absorbed; I assume the tree-buffered environment is the normal environment. If I assume this, then the trees appear as passive ornaments adapted to this pleasant place. I rarely realize how much power would roar through this canyon if it were not for the trees. .

The trees are doing the same thing in Aspen Canyon that the mats of moss are doing high in the Rockies. They are shifting and maintaining the relative balances that allow soil and moisture to accumulate. Aspen Canyon is an example of an upward spiral in which life nourishes the soil and the soil nourishes life.

⌒

Sand Canyon, unfortunately, spirals in the opposite direction. Aspen Canyon was fenced off from livestock, but in Sand Canyon only the areas around the cliff dwellings are fenced off. Cattle roam everywhere else, eating plants faster than they can grow. Normally, such a concentration of grazing animals would nourish a presence of mountain lions but all the lions have been shot.

The native grasses were eaten long ago. Cheat grass (from Europe) survives because after it dries in the summer, it is too stickery for the cows to eat. However, its roots do not bind the sand into soil as well as the native grasses did. The falling water table has withered the trees that once shaded and mulched the sandy ground. A few groves of oaks and box elders survive at the base of the canyon walls but the main expanse of the canyon floor is dominated by the growing arroyo, cheat grass, and cow dung. Phoebes catch the flies attracted by the dung while ravens turn over the dung in search of beetles. The stream, a few inches deep, meanders along the arroyo bottom past innumerable islands of cow dung. As the dung dissolves into the stream, the fertility within this canyon flows away.

With fewer plants growing, the cattle must graze more heavily. Cattle must cover more ground in their search for food. Each time a cow clambers up the steep, sandy banks of the arroyo, its hooves push a bit of the terrace down into the arroyo. Heavy hooves cut trails wherever cattle follow one another across the level terraces. Storm run-off converges upon these smooth, straight trails and erodes them into gullies. As these gullies dissect the terraces into smaller sections, less level land remains to absorb the rain. More of the rain runs off, which increases the erosive power converging within the arroyo. The arroyo cuts deeper, draining the water table lower. Water that once rose through plants now flows down along the bottom of the arroyo.

Once upon a time, soil and water accumulated within this canyon, nourishing the aspen with which the cliff dwellers roofed their rooms. But then relative balances shifted. An arroyo formed and withered the emerald canyon. The cliff dwellers were forced to leave. After they left, the balances shifted back. The arroyo filled in, the water table rose, and trees returned. Now the overgrazing cattle have shifted the relative balance once again and a new arroyo drains the canyon of its possibilities.

Depending on the relative balances in the flows of water and soil, this canyon can become a shady, rustling emerald-green aspen wood or a dung-filled desert. Either is possible. As I understand the implications of balance more, Aspen Canyon and Sand Canyon become symbols for this Earth. Our planet can be a green jewel fertile with possibilities or it can be a harsh wasteland drained of possibilities. Our Earth can grow either way. Its direction depends on the relative balances of the flows that nourish Gaia. Life has the power to shift those balances in either direction.

I am part of life too. When I sit within the healing peace of Aspen Canyon, the emerald forests of Gaia invite me to become a conscious participant in the creation of this healing peace and beauty. I want to accept the invitation, but I am not sure how. When I sit within Sand Canyon, the slipping soil and withering plants cry out to my heart for help. But I do not know how to help. What can one person do?

The Storms

⌒

OVER THE NEXT FEW MONTHS, I searched for some way to help Sand Canyon. I built tiny stone check dams on the mesas and scattered cottonwood seeds within the arroyo. In August, the traditional time for thunderstorms, I went out to Sand Canyon for my final ten-day tour of duty.

Normally the bone-dry cliff dwellings had no smell. But this summer had been abundantly wet; the damp air released the aroma of smoke from rocks blackened by cook fires seven hundred years ago. The town smelled freshly abandoned.

The canyon also appeared fresh, because all the cattle had been driven out in July for branding. The storms began shortly thereafter and now quicksand prevented the cattle from coming back up the canyon. For more than a month, the canyon had received abundant rain and no livestock. Grass and flowers grew thick. Wild roses sprouted from chewed-off stalks. I had never seen Sand Canyon more beautiful. How easily it could grow in beauty and possibilities if only the downward spiral of overgrazing and erosion could be reversed.

The rains had been so heavy this summer, however, that run-off from a small waterfall was eroding a gully between the ranger residence and the cliff dwellings. This run-off, flowing fifty yards across the terrace and then plunging down the steep sandy bank of the arroyo, would eventually cut this large terrace in half. I had no idea how to heal the canyon's large arroyo but stopping the erosion of this small gully felt like an appropriate challenge. I built a series of check dams in the gully with wooden boards.

After a few days of good weather, a storm came. Waterfalls poured off the cliffs. The stream in the arroyo swelled to a flood. I went out to watch my check dams. Run-off from the waterfall was just beginning to flow across the terrace. The front of that flow encountered my first board, quietly pooled up behind it, overflowed, and continued to the next check dam. I followed the stream as it moved across the terrace. The stream paused to pool up behind each board. Good, my dams were slowing the run-off. I hoped that water-carried sand would drop out in the slack water behind each dam and fill in the gully.

Anyone who has washed a car and watched the water flow down the driveway and along the street gutter knows that the probing front edge of the water moves slowly along the dry gutter. The water that follows flows deeper and much faster. When I returned to the upper check dams, I found brown torrents plunging over them. The check dams were concentrating the stream's energy into turbulent plunges that pounded at the base of each check dam. Within minutes, the dams had washed out.

Only one check dam held. It happened to be a board that stuck up above the gully. Therefore, most of the run-off flowed around the check dam rather than over it. Also, the slope of the terrace at that point just happened to direct this water away from the gully to new paths on either side. Inadvertently, my dam had split the torrent of water into three streams.

The change in the flow of water was dramatic. Water within the narrow, smooth gully had encountered very little frictional resistance, so its energy went into speed, power, and erosion. But the three channels, two of which were broad, shallow, and filled with cheat grass, possessed far more surface. Overcoming the frictional resistance of that greater surface consumed most of the run-off's energy. The brown water lost the energy needed to transport sand and dropped its load where the torrent diverged into three slower, gentler streams.

The powerful effect of this divergence suggested a strategy. I followed each stream across the terrace, looking for further opportunities to split it. Each stream became two, then four, eight . . . Each split caused the water to flow more slowly, giving time for more of the run-off to soak into the sandy soil. Splitting grew easier as the broadening runoff flowed across the level terrace. I simply scratched a V into the sand and a rivulet forked into the two scratch marks.

The storm ended. None of the run-off had reached the edge of the terrace. All of it had soaked in.

But the next day, the biggest storm I'd ever seen in the canyon hit. On a scale of one to ten, this storm was a ten. The lightning was directly overhead. I assumed that the seven hundred-foot cliffs acted as lightning rods, so I felt safe. The lightning exploded the air. The banging thunder smashed against the canyon walls and rebounded in vast waves of echoes. These echoes grew fainter as the main blast of thunder bounced up the canyon. And then the series of reverberating booms grew louder. The head of the canyon two miles away had reflected the shock wave of thunder back downcanyon. Louder and louder the returning rumbles grew, then a large muffled boom as the energy surged by me, and then receding booms as the main shock wave moved downcanyon. About a mile downcanyon, the thunder crashed against a sharp turn in the canyon. Much of its energy was reflected back toward me. Again the sound crescendoed as the echoes swept past and then receded upcanyon again. Whether that thunder's rumbling energy would return a third time I do not know, for another lightning bolt sent a fresh wave of sound sloshing back and forth within the vibrating canyon.

All around me were waterfalls. Not postcard-pretty streams of white mist cascading over the cliffs, but dirt-brown floods being flushed down the cliffs. I shouted encouragement to my check dam as I shoveled away the accumulating deposit of sand that was burying the side channels. Then down across the terrace I went, searching for new places to lead the run-off. I felt like an ancient Egyptian leading the Nile flood onto the fields. The run-off, now split into hundreds of tiny streams, advanced only a foot a minute across the terrace. Yet, as the downpour continued, the relentless runoff slowly pushed me closer and closer to the edge of the arroyo. The V's I drew in the sand were now only a yard from the edge. I had to be careful out there, for undermined sections of the terrace were cracking off with muffled ker-whumps and sliding into the flood. Each collapse would partially dam the flood but the brown water swirled the tons of sand away in seconds.

I gazed down into the massive flood. Slow eddies of brown water swirled off to the side of the main current. I recognized each eddy as a place where, on sunny non-flood days, a mound of sand rose above the arroyo floor. Now I understood the origin of those mounds of sand. Sand drops out wherever the dirty brown flood is slowed by an eddy.

I looked up at the cliffs and discovered that the color of the cliffs fit with the patterns of the rain. Parts of the cliff that were grayish-green with lichens were damp with rain. Parts of the cliff that had been streaked with black and red mineral stains had water oozing precisely down each streak. If a streak split in two, the ooze of water also did. And cliff sections that had the dusty sandy color of unweathered sandstone were dry—even in the midst of this storm. That dusty color revealed every overhang in the canyon.

A massive storm shapes the land more than the many months between storms. All around I could watch the formation of details I had never noticed before. The canyon was awash with patterns that had been invisible in the summer Sun. Information and understanding flooded my brain.

In the midst of this adrenaline rush, I realized I was having the time of my life. Interacting with the storm's intense energy was a blast of fun. Some war veterans have said they felt most alive in the midst of combat. I could understand that now. Unfortunately, war destroys so much. Its short-term thrill for the survivors can never balance its long-term destruction and misery. But this moment in the canyon was in the service of life. Rather than battling and destroying other humans, I was battling erosion. My rain-drenched body was exerting itself beyond its normal limits. I felt great!

The sound of rain pummeling the ground slackened. I knew then I had won the battle. I pushed myself to oppose the forward movement of the run-off for a few more minutes. The rain stopped and the only sound was the roar of the waterfalls and the flood in the arroyo. The run-off soaked into the sandy terrace. Within fifteen minutes, warm sunlight sent mists rising into the blue sky. The waterfalls gentled into clear water rippling down the cliffs with splashing sounds. Birds sang. The canyon was exquisitely beautiful, more beautiful than any place I had ever seen, for I was seeing with eyes of exhilaration. I had been able to keep ninety-nine percent of a massive onslaught of run-off on the terrace with my divergences. Sand had been deposited on the terrace rather than eroded from it. I had won the battle!

⌒

The next day was sunny. I did some repair work on top of the house. Around eleven o'clock, a small storm came in. I went onto the terrace to do battle, but my divergences were already in place and I handled the run-off easily.

At two o'clock, another storm arrived; large enough to send me out in the rain, large enough to send another flood down the canyon, but easily controllable up on the terrace. The adrenaline rush of yesterday was giving way to the calm of confident competency.

And then, at four o'clock, the Monster Storm arrived. On a scale of one to ten, this storm was a twenty.

I sent the run-off into every area I could, but run-off was pouring over the edge all along the terrace. I stood near the edge of the arroyo and watched a tremendous piece of terrace slide into the flood. There was no ker-whump because the raging torrent within the arroyo carried away the earth as fast as it slid in. The whole thing, bushes still binding their chunks of earth together, descended the slope and disappeared.

After about forty-five minutes, I heard that magic sound of pounding rain relenting. Thankfully, I redoubled my efforts knowing that soon the run-off would subside. But two minutes later, the full fury of the storm hit. Now the monster storm revealed its full power. Everything intensified. The rain pounded so hard that the sandy soil of the terrace flowed away before my eyes. I found myself crying to the storm to stop, please stop. Rivers a foot deep surged across the terrace. I looked up to see one of my favorite waterfalls and was staggered to see that the entire cliff face, one hundred feet across, was a waterfall.

There came a time of such sustained intensity that I gave up. I put down my tool and went to see the cliff dwelling. Four massive waterfalls crashed in front of the alcove. A brown cloud of muddy mist veiled the town. The canyon vibrated with pounding waterfalls. The storm pounded humility into my resigned mind. How pretentious were yesterday's feelings of "winning." Nature has the power to easily overwhelm and wash away my work.

I stared across the arroyo at the run-off that was cascading down the opposite bank. The entire bank was washing away, but the areas held together by grass were eroding more slowly than the unprotected bare areas. This slower erosion turned the clumps of grass into high points that diverged the run-off around them. Many clumps eventually washed down the slope and disappeared in the brown flood below. Yet for as long as each clump of grass remained, it created a divergence that reduced the energy of the cascade. Even if the grass washed away, it had reduced erosion during the time it stood. If those plants had not been growing on the side of the arroyo, the erosion would have been worse.

I am like the grass, I thought. My efforts prevent the erosion from being worse. Even if the flood washes away my efforts, my resistance will have absorbed some of the flood's energy and lessened the erosion that otherwise would have happened. Whether my efforts are enough to "win" depends upon the force I oppose. If the force is small enough, I shall "win." If it is large enough, I "lose". To be proud of "winning" is to be proud of encountering a force smaller than myself. I should forget about "winning" and, like the grass, simply resist the erosion.

I returned to my work. Twenty minutes later, the pounding rain subsided. So accustomed to that pounding had I become that its slackening sounded like stillness even though the waterfalls still shook the bedrock.

⌒

After the storm I went up into the cliff dwelling to check the streaks on the alcove's ceiling. The streaks of mineral stain form an accumulated record of all the storms since this alcove formed; the larger the storm, the farther down each streak the rainwater oozes. The water from this storm extended beyond every single stain line. It had been a once-in-many-centuries storm.

Seven miles away, park headquarters had a beautiful, blue-sky afternoon. Rangers had seen a huge thunderhead out over the canyon, but it had been solitary. All that power had been within a single cloud.

Diverging

A FEW DAYS LATER, I was driving toward the suburbs of Los Angeles to teach at an elementary school. Upon arrival, I found that the school was nearly surrounded by a huge, overgrazed field. Gullies six feet deep caught my eye. Teachers told me that sometimes enough run-off came from that field to flood the school grounds. El Niño happened that winter; storm after storm dropped thirty-five inches in five months, giving me abundant opportunities to continue to experiment with diverging run-off.

When the storms came, I went up into the fields with my shovel, searching for places to create divergences. My technique consisted of shoveling enough sod into a channel to form a dam. This dam had to be tall enough to force the water to flow around it onto a new path rather than over it. The dam had to be thick enough to hold back the torrent that it opposed. Building these dams required lots of sod. I felt badly about the pockmarked field that I created when I dug out hunks of sod.

Because of the large effort required, I could build only a few of these dams. In order to have the most impact, I built the dams in the lower main channels. These dams survived the first small storms, giving me hope that my work was effective. But the first large storm washed them away. Too much erosive power flowed in these lower channels. I was forced to retreat to the smaller channels near the top of the drainage, where run-off was just beginning to converge its power. Up there, in channels a few inches wide, my dams survived.

But little erosion occurred up there. Having to work so far upstream of the gullies made me aware of how limited my power was. I found myself wishing for a bulldozer with enough power to push significant dams into those eroding gullies. But all I had was a shovel and a technique for diverging water. I resigned myself to the smaller channels. At least their abundance offered me hundreds of opportunities to practice my technique.

And as I practiced, things began to happen.

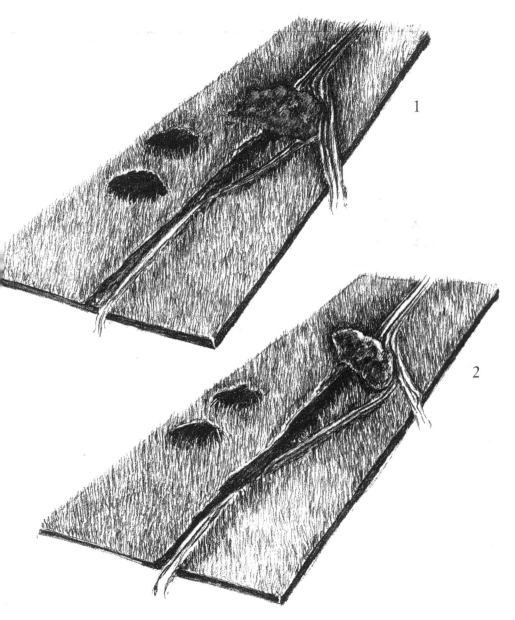

My divergences evolved from opposing the flow of water to leading the water onto new paths.

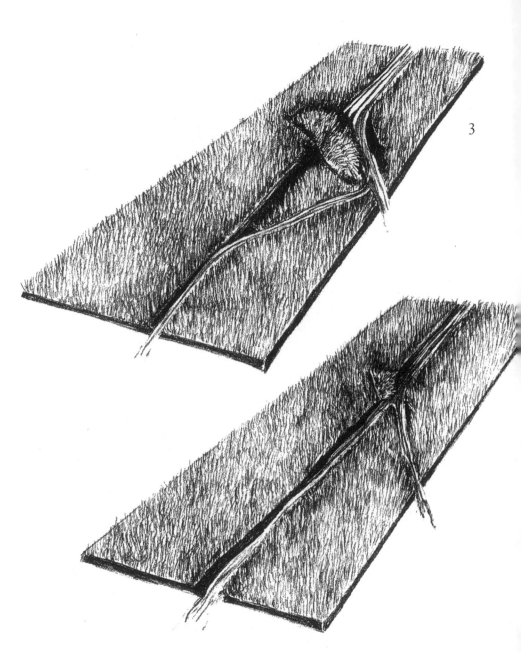

3

My divergences grew more efficient. I had built my first dams straight across the channel, forcing the water to stop, pool up, and turn to the side (see illustration 1). These sudden stops and sharp turns created turbulent energy that wore away dams, so the dams had to be massive.

Yet eventually I realized that all I was trying to do with these dams was turn some of the run-off onto a new path. I did not have to stop the entire flow of water to do that. Water flows more smoothly around gradual curves. I changed my dams so that they were angled instead of straight across the channel (2).

The momentum that previously carried water over my dams now carried some of the water over the bank onto a new path. This new design used the water's momentum instead of trying to oppose it.

This change in design led to another change. Previously, my only strategy had been to raise a dam. But if I also used my shovel to lower the bank where the turning water overflowed, then more run-off would flow onto the new path (3). Lowering the bank a few inches turned out to be much more effective and easier than building up the entire dam a few inches.

Leading the water with a channel was easier than forcing the water with a dam. In fact, if I built the channel before starting the dam, my dam did not have to be as large, because the turning water didn't push against the dam as much. This discovery felt profound and rich with allegory. Offer a new path before opposing the old path.

⌒

As I practiced, I learned that dams and channels in some places had no effect while structures in other places had powerful effects. Precise location was more effective than large size. I learned how ripples on the surface of the run-off could guide my shovel precisely to the most powerful places. This precision allowed me to use a narrower, lighter shovel. The narrower blade required less energy to push through the sod. The lighter shovel required less energy to carry. The work of building divergences grew easier.

As I concentrated on precision, I learned that my dams did not have to extend across the main channel (4). All I needed to turn the water's momentum toward the new channel was a partial dam angling out from the opposite bank upstream of the new channel. I could build this structure using just the sod excavated from the new channel. Such a structure did not lead all the water onto the new path, but all I wanted was to split the stream. My structures simply offered the water a second path to follow. Although some of the water rushed on, part of it diverged onto a new path, which created a gentling effect on both paths.

Now I was moving only a few pieces of sod upstream a few feet from one bank to the other side of the channel. No unsightly holes pockmarked the surrounding fields. No longer was I lugging heavy pieces of sod across the field. No massive dams loomed within a stream channel. The gentle curve of low sod structures turning water smoothly toward new paths looked natural. My efforts became invisible to the casual eye.

~~

The way this work evolved delighted me. I began the work with an awkward design, random actions, and assumptions of limited possibilities. I did some work and the results altered the way I did the work next time. Practice initiated a spiral of learning between the fields and myself. My structures evolved from opposing the flow of water to turning and leading the water onto new paths. These structures fit better within the flow of water and accomplished more with less effort. Because of the wisdom evolving within the design, I could now make more divergences with the same amount of energy and time. The work was acquiring possibilities.

This work reminded me of the process of evolution. Tiny changes create opportunities for other tiny changes. Over time, what seemed impossible becomes possible. Each time I discover a new possibility created by my work, my spirit begins singing, "Don't wait until there is a clear path to the goal. Begin. Doing the work will help create the path."

Allies Emerge

*I*T WAS IMPOSSIBLE TO DIVERGE run-off within the gullies, because the water down there was confined between towering banks. And I assumed I could do nothing for the gullies when I had to retreat to the small channels upstream of them. Yet as my upstream divergences proliferated, something unexpected happened.

I discovered it in my second year at the school. A large storm had poured all night. Night storms usually end in the morning, so I hurried out in the darkness. I wanted to be up at the headwaters of the drainage when the storm-clouded dawn gave enough light to work. As I cut across the fields in the dark, I stepped into a large stream of run-off in a grass camouflaged channel I had never noticed before. I thought I knew every channel in these fields. What was this stream doing here? Where was its water coming from?

I followed this mystery upstream and discovered that its source was a year's accumulation of my divergences, which had led much of the run-off so far away from the main channel that the water now flowed across a subtle divide into an abandoned channel. Water that had previously cascaded into the gully now flowed smoothly and quietly along this grassy channel, completely avoiding the gullies.

I hadn't realized that with just a shovel I could lead water into a new drainage. Suddenly my work acquired a new strategy with unknown possibilities. I could do something about the gullies. As I built more divergences over the years, I came upon more of these opportunities. I was delighted by each discovery of a hidden channel, because it allowed me to lead run-off from an eroding area into a healthy area. Yet the channels puzzled me. Why were they so conveniently located? As I walked along them during storms, I began to understand.

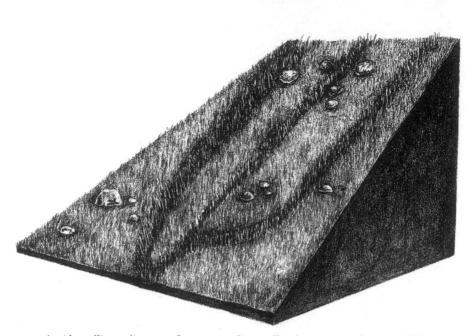

As side gullies radiate out from an eroding gully, they capture the run-off flowing in other small drainages.

Once upon a time, before the gully formed, run-off did not converge as quickly. It flowed gently along many subtle, parallel channels rather than in one large gully. However, when overgrazing caused more of the rain to run off, erosion began to deepen one of the channels. As side gullies radiated from this gully, they cut across other channels and diverted their flow of water into the gully.

Small channels are abandoned as side gullies capture their source of water. The deepening gully "bends" run-off toward it. Water that once flowed parallel to the eroding channel now enters the gully higher upstream. Run-off converges in the gully faster than it did previously. This increases the power of water flowing through the gully, which causes further deepening, which causes longer side gullies, which causes more run-off to be "bent" toward the gully, which converges more power within the gully. Through this spiral, both a gully and the power flowing through it grow.

The abandonment of subtle channels is part of the process of erosion. But the abandoned channels are still there, and they can emerge as powerful allies in reversing the erosive spiral. Understanding how these channels were abandoned helped me locate more of them. When I could divert water back into these channels, I felt like I was reversing the

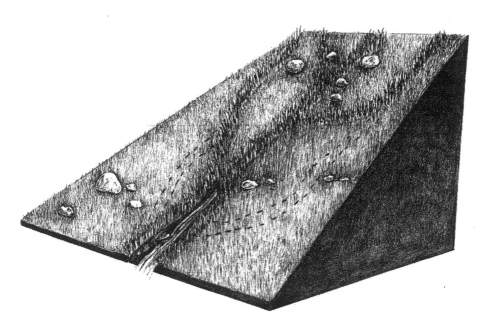

These gentle swales are left abandoned off to the side of the deepening gully.

process of erosion, undoing its damage. I began to shape my divergences consciously so they led the run-off around the gullies toward open, level grassy areas where the water would spread out, slow down, and soak in.

⌒

Willows began to sprout in some gullies where willows had not grown before. The willow saplings would help slow the run-off and provide nesting sites for insects and birds. I came to realize that the places where erosion was most intense were also the places where growth could be most lush, because as a gully grew deeper, it also drew closer to the water table. Plants within the gully could tap into a source of water unavailable to plants up above. When run-off stopped scouring the gullies, the gully bottoms became promising sites for drifting seeds.

In the fourth year, a migrating flock of geese visited the fields and left behind thousands of rich, green, nitrogen-filled droppings to fertilize the growing grass. I had never seen geese in the fields before. Were they responding to my work? Sand Canyon had once hosted ducks and geese. Those geese had left when the water table had dropped, but geese can also return.

I was fascinated and delighted to see how the spiraling changes that occur with erosion can develop in the other direction. In Sand Canyon, the arroyo had drained the water table. As the water table dropped, the plants had withered. Dying plants provided less mulch to cover and protect the soil. The rain pounded the exposed ground and more of the rain ran off to swell the erosive power flowing within the arroyo. The arroyo grew deeper, which drained the water table still lower.

But in the school fields, more of the rain that would have run off was now soaking in, and the water table was rising. Life responded; new plants appeared and other plants expanded their range. Beautiful mini-marshes of wild mustard and radish appeared at the lower end of each gully in areas that had been bare dirt when I first came. As plants grew more abundantly, their leaves protected more of the ground from the Sun and pounding rain. The protected soil could absorb more of the rain, which raised the water table and nourished more plants. Less rain ran off to converge in the gully.

In Sand Canyon, I saw possibilities draining away from the land. Here in the fields, I saw possibilities rising. An image formed of cause-and-effect relationships acting like teeter-totters. A shift in relative balances causes sequences of cause-and-effect to tilt to the other direction. Downward spirals of erosion reverse direction and become upward spirals of growth. Processes I had previously cursed magically transform into allies.

I no longer saw myself confronting and halting erosion single-handedly. I began to see my work as that of shifting balances—little balances—wherever I encountered the opportunity. Whenever a balance shifts, an enemy will become an ally to help me with the work.

Each walk in the fields became alive with anticipation. What new ally might I meet? What unimagined opportunity might that ally make possible? Each unpredictable discovery of an unimagined possibility left me feeling delightfully unsure of what was possible and what was impossible. The freshness of this delight made me realize that for years I had practiced looking for reasons why hope was impossible. Over the years, I had practiced becoming increasingly cynical. My cynical perceptions of the world had limited my interactions with the world in ways that confirmed and nourished my cynical perception. I acted less and doubted more. My energy had become increasingly bound up in constraining my hopes and criticizing the misdeeds of others.

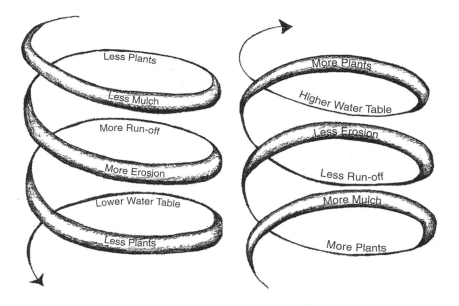

The downward spiral of erosion can reverse to become an upward spiral of healing.

But participating in Gaia's unimagined possibilities released my energy for action. I lost interest in deciding what was impossible and became more interested in what was possible. My cynical mutter of "What can one person do?" transformed into a wondering murmur of "What can one person do?" The downward spiral of cynicism reversed and rose as the upward spiral of hope. I acted and accomplished far more when I was hopeful than when I was cynical.

My spirit was healing. My actions increasingly resonated with my dreams. I felt what it was like to participate in a process that is billions of years old and that is capable of extending billions of years into the future. I can become a mobile, conscious part of a process that brings impossibilities into reality. The future is open-ended, nourished by dreams, hope, and work. This work was healing me as much as it was healing the fields. This made sense in a strange way because I, too, was part of the life in those fields. A spiral of healing joined us.

The Invisible Power

THE OVERGRAZED FIELDS near the school had many bare patches of compacted dirt that were almost as hard as rock. I could not push a shovel blade into them. Plants could not root there. Even the rain could not soak in there. After a storm, the ground looked wet but if I scratched it with my shovel, chalky dry dirt lay just beneath the surface.

Slowly, however, plants were encroaching on these hostile areas by rooting in the softer ground beyond and sending leafy, viny stems out over the barren ground. This covering of stems and leaves shaded the ground and trapped windblown dust and dead leaves. This material held some of the rain long enough to let it soak and swell the ground. When I looked beneath the viny stems, I saw bugs and damp, brown soil. The compacted dirt was softening. Someday plants would be able to root there and advance their viny stems farther into the bare patch. This encroachment of life reminded me of the moss mats spreading over the granite bedrock.

Watching life transform this compacted dirt into soil made me aware of how unusual soil really is. If I put dirt, water, and air into a bottle and shake it, there will be a bubbly swirl of muddy water, then the air will quickly rise out of the water and the dirt will gradually settle to the bottom. Left to themselves, earth, water, and air will separate. This separation happens all the time around us. Gravity collapses tunnels, compresses the soil, and squeezes out the air spaces that absorb the rain. Left to itself, soil will compress and form an abrupt, barren edge with the air.

However, life uses its energy to transform this abrupt edge into a gradient, a mix of earth, moisture, and air a few or many inches deep. Plants breathe in gases from the sky, absorb minerals and moisture from the earth, and mix earth, sky, and water together within their bodies. The plants also nourish a billion scratchers and burrowers. Birds fluff the topsoil when they scratch in the mulch, searching for seeds. Tunnel-digging gophers excavate compacted subsoil and heap it loosely onto the surface. Their tunnels allow run-off to flow deep into the ground. Worms do the same thing on a smaller, more abundant scale. Their tunnels allow air to penetrate deep beneath the Earth's surface.

At season's end, the plants die and bow to the ground in a great folding together of earth and sky. Gravity tamps the withered stems and abandoned spider webs into a dense sponge. Next winter, after each storm, I will squoosh through water an inch deep held stationary by this thick, grassy sponge. More of the slowly flowing run-off will soak in and nourish more growth, more mixing.

⌒

Life's mixing of earth and sky opens the Earth to the rain. When I first came to the fields, most of the rainwater ran off toward the sea, using its power to carry soil away with it. But now most of the rain soaks into the ground. The rain still contains power, but the power expresses itself through a different work. The power softens and swells the Earth, forms soil, moistens the chemistry of life. The rain's power to wash away all that stands above sea level has been absorbed and transformed into the power to nourish all life above sea level.

The spiral of erosion reverses itself and becomes a great upward spiral: Life mixes earth and atmosphere into absorbent soil; this soil absorbs more of the rain; the moist soil nourishes more life; and more life mixes still more of the earth and atmosphere into soil. Each small change leads to other small changes.

As the days grow longer and warmer, the slopes bring forth sprouting plants by the billions. These plants draw earth, water, sky, and Sun into their bodies to form future soil. Roots and worms push through the ground and wedge the soil upward. This uprising is unstoppable. As I watch the thickening soil engulf rocks and old boards, I see that life possesses the power to actually raise the surface of the Earth.

⌒

The Invisible Power   155

And yet this power is almost invisible. Erosion's power is easy to see, because we see it concentrated within a few gullies during the few hours of a flood. Life's power, on the other hand, is spread over all the slopes and over many weeks of growth. Life's power is so abundantly diffused through space and time that I rarely realize its magnitude. The great paradox underlying Gaia is that her enormous, creative power is invisible.

To comprehend that power, we need to multiply little changes by trillions of lives and millions of years. A grass blade swaying in the wind absorbs an infinitesimally small amount of the wind's finite power, but a billion grass blades accumulate enough power to wedge the wind away from the soil. If winds could touch the soil, the soil would be blown away as it was in the Dust Bowl. The power within one grass blade multiplied over millions of acres becomes a power sufficient to create and protect the fertile soils of the prairie. However, when we look for this power, all we see are grass blades tossed by the wind. Any appearance of power has been dissipated into a great number of seemingly insignificant changes.

I walked into the fields after a spring storm. The run-off had pushed down the long grasses growing in the channels. The bent-over grasses swayed as the current flowed along them. The current's influence on the grass was easy to see. But the remarkable quietness of the run-off called my attention to the influence the grass was having on the current. The grass swayed because it was absorbing the turbulent swirls of energy within the current. By absorbing the water's noisy, erosive energy, the grass kept the run-off flowing smoothly, quietly, and silt-free. The power of erosion is easily heard. Yet quietness is also an expression of power, a power that is harder to hear.

The diffuse, easily overlooked power of Gaia does not fit the image of power I learned as a child. I imagined power as concentrated and obvious like the power that roars down a gully during a storm. Concentrated power was the kind of power I desired as a child and the kind I desired when I wished for bulldozers with which to dam the gullies.

Interestingly, the concentrated power of bulldozers did come to the fields. Truckloads of dirt from a large construction project were dumped into the gullies of the adjoining field. A bulldozer pushed and compacted the dirt into big, thick dams. When the rains came, all the run-off pooled up behind the dams and erosion ceased downstream. I leaned on my shovel and sighed longingly.

A few more storms came, and the pools filled up and overflowed. The overflowing water quickly cut through the massive, earthen dams and erosion resumed as before. The larger the attempted change, the larger the resisting force. The concentrated power of a bulldozer could not do what I had thought. If anything, the heavy bulldozer made the erosion worse by compacting the ground around the gullies so that even more rain ran off.

In contrast to the dams of the bulldozer, thousands of tiny inch-high dams formed spontaneously during each storm. These dams, made of dead grass blades and other things that float, contoured the slopes perfectly and held back shallow pools of water. Line after line of these dams and ponds often terraced a slope, like a series of miniature rice paddies.

The stability of these flimsy dams fascinated me. If I broke one of the dams, the water in its pond began to flow through the breach and carry floating debris to the breach. Because of surface adhesion, this material stuck to the broken ends of the dam. The breach quickly clotted up.

If there was a low spot on the dam, the water overflowed there. The floating debris adhered there and built up that low section. The moment that low spot was raised level with the rest of the dam, no more water flowed that way, so there was no more buildup. That is why these "accidental" dams were so remarkably level.

If the water flowed around the end of the dam, the floating material drifted to that end, adhered there, and lengthened the dam along the contour of the slope. The dam rose and extended itself uniformly until the water oozed throughout the dam.

These "Gaia dams," as my wife named them, transform a narrow rivulet into a spread-out ooze. A series of ponds break the momentum of the run-off. Water detained by the dams soaks into the ground rather than running off to converge in the main channels. After the storm, the run-off subsides. The dams deflate and dry into easily overlooked strands of dried plant material contouring the slopes. Gaia dams form everywhere—on grasslands, in forests, even in neighborhood street gutters (though the street sweepers keep swishing them away). They remind me that creating many small changes is more sustainable than trying to impose a few, large changes.

When I began my work in the fields, I assumed I had to work in the eroded gullies and confront the torrents directly. But I learned that helping the soil absorb the rain was more effective than opposing the concentrated power of rushing run-off. If the soil absorbed the rain, the power of erosion never formed in the first place. The most powerful place for healing was not in the gullies but where raindrops first touched the Earth.

I do not work alone. I am surrounded by Gaia's invisible power. A billion roots hold soil upon the slopes and the soil holds the rain. Without the maintaining energy of life, the soil would slide and wash away, springs would run dry, and rivers would dwindle. Without plants, oxygen would not be replenished as it combined with elements of the Earth and faded from the atmosphere. Our Earth's environment is as dependent on its life as life is dependent on its environment. This spiraling miracle of interdependency is the heart of Gaia. I feel deep gratitude and humility toward all the "lower" forms of life. Without their efforts, "our" environment would slip back toward the primal environment and our existence would become impossible.

The Test

⌒

I SIT IN THE FIELDS beside a diversion flowing with run-off, which leads water away from the gully out onto the slopes. I contemplate a mystery that I can best explain with the aid of this book. Keep the book open to this page (but not opened all the way flat). Hold it this way in front of you. Now angle the open book toward you until Point 1 is just a little bit higher up in the air than Point 2.

In this position, the book models a drainage. Each page is one of the slopes draining toward the drainage that runs down the center. We'll pretend that the gutter where they come together is a gully. The diagonal line going across the page is my diversion leading run-off away from the gully.

If I hadn't built the diversion, the water would have flowed quickly down the gully to the bottom of the page. However, because of the diversion, some of the water now flows along the line across the page. Water flowing along that line will also be flowing downhill (if you are holding the book correctly), so no violation of physical law is involved.

What fascinates me is that the water that flows in the divergence ends up high above where it would have if I hadn't built that divergence. It's as if water at Point A near the bottom of the book flowed back up to Point B. That *would* be a violation of physical law. It doesn't happen that way and yet the consequence is the same. The more it rains, the more water "flows up."

On a larger scale, now imagine that instead of doing work, I had done nothing and then, after many years, tried to replace the topsoil and water that had flowed away. I imagine trucks sucking up water from downstream and lumbering heavily across the soft fields, spraying water behind them. I imagine bulldozers scooping up the deposits of eroded silt in the nearby estuary. Complex machinery would separate the silt from the salt of the estuary's brackish water. Trucks would then haul the dirt up and dump it in the fields, where bulldozers would spread it over the ground. The use of such heavy equipment and so much energy would look like real work. And yet, walking lightly with a shovel, I achieved a better result by reducing the loss of water and soil in the first place.

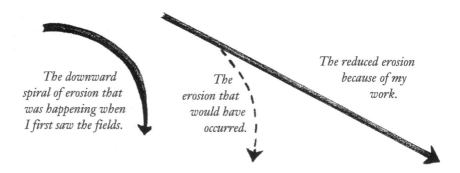

The downward spiral of erosion that was happening when I first saw the fields.

The erosion that would have occurred.

The reduced erosion because of my work.

My work, moreover, has done more than just reduce the outflow of rainwater and soil from these fields. My work has increased the inflow of energy. As balances shift and erosion gives way to healing, plants colonize bare patches of dirt. Previously, those bright lifeless surfaces reflected sunlight. In a thousandth of a second, the Sun's energy was back in space, streaking away from the earth that had rejected its gift of possibilities. However, as plants cover the reflective dirt with absorbent green, more of the Sun's gift of energy enters the cycles of life.

This energy helps more leaves grow which will absorb even more energy. This energy allows the plants to mix more of the earth and air together so that more rain will be absorbed and more soil will form. Once begun, the upward spiral can maintain itself by absorbing more of the sunlight and rainwater. No additional work is needed from me. A downward spiral has become an upward spiral.

By shifting relative balances, a downward spiral becomes a sunlight-powered upward spiral.

Year after year my divergences alter the flows of water, soil, and energy. The longer my works remain in place, the more effects they will accumulate. (This means that the sooner I start my work, the more powerful it will be.) The difference between what is happening and what would have happened grows greater with every sunny day and every passing storm. At some point this difference will grow greater than the energy I used in building my divergences. The accumulating amount of erosion that does not happen will become greater than the work I did. As a result, the world will have more possibilities because of my work than it would have had without it.

Seven years earlier when I had sat in the desert beside the dead deer, I thought the Second Law of Thermodynamics prevented the accumulation of energy. I assumed that the Second Law meant that my actions could only decrease possibilities and that my life was limited to consuming the possibilities of this world. That assumption had burdened my spirit. This work of erosion control has released me from that burden by making me aware of the two levels of energy flow.

The flow of energy is like the flow of water. Even though water can flow only downhill, water can accumulate and rise in a bathtub. Even though the Second Law of Thermodynamics requires that energy on the individual level must flow "down," energy can accumulate on the group level if energy inflow is greater than energy outflow. There are always two ways to shift a relative balance. I can decrease the outflow (such as by reducing erosion) and I can increase the inflow (such as by helping plants cover the reflective ground with sunlight-absorbing surfaces).

If the relative balance can be shifted, then downward spirals can reverse and become sunshine-powered upward spirals that alter the land in ways that capture more sunshine to power other upward spirals. The work grows on itself like compound interest. As long as the Sun's energy flows upon this Earth, our world can increase in possibilities and we can be part of its growth. Though such growth is slow, it can be sustained for hundreds of millions of years. My life can be more than a consumption of possibilities.

One spring day when the fields were at maximum green, I sat by a place that had allowed an impressive series of divergences. Grasses were now colonizing what had once been an expanse of bare dirt. My work had made possible that grass. A bug fed on one of the grass stems. Had my work helped create this bug? Just then I heard a bird sing. Birds raise their babies on insects. Had my work nourished that song?

I felt a resonance with life. Just as other lives were helping me in my work so my work was helping them in their lives. We were reinforcing one another. Almost everything in this field might have been nourished by my work. Even the clouds above were replenished, in part, by the moisture transpired by this grass. The rain I retained in the fields, instead of running off to the sea, might now fall as snow on distant mountains and water mats of moss this summer. As the traditional boundaries between myself and the world became confused, I felt myself Fit with the world.

As I reflect on this sense of Fit, I begin seeing the Second Law of Thermodynamics as posing a test to each evolving species. "Can you find a path that does not consume possibilities faster than they are created?" If a species consumes possibilities faster than they are created, then its environment will decrease in possibilities and become less capable of supporting that species. In fact, a reward will emerge for any other lifeform that can develop a way to diminish this too-consuming species. The species will encounter increasing resistance. The test is simple but immutable. If a species cannot pass the test, it will not endure.

We must consume possibilities. We must harvest energy from other parts of the greater system. The test does not forbid that. What the test requires is maintaining a relative balance. The simplest strategy is to reduce the amount of energy and resources consumed. This is an ancient, venerable path that has shaped the bodies and behavior of practically every living thing. The hollowness of bird bones. The increasing distance between nodes as a grass stem tapers. The way insect larvae in fast-moving streams fit in the boundary layer between rock and current. The living world vibrates with this strategy.

The fields of Gaia, however, have taught me an additional strategy to help pass the test. We can use part of the energy that we harvest to loop back "upstream" and do work that alters and enhances the flows upon which our survival depends.

Worms do the work of wedging the ground upward so that air, rain, and therefore roots can penetrate deeper into the soil and create more food for the worms. Dying streamside trees fall downslope across the stream, forming dams where pools fill with gravel and deepen the soil and water table so the trees' descendants can grow more easily. Beaver build dams that slow water and trap nutrients. Like a balloon over a faucet, these dams inflate the stream into a pond with a circumference edged with succulent willows. Salmon, at the end of their life, fertilize with their bodies the trees that kept the stream shaded and cold for them as fingerlings and will keep it cold for their offspring that will emerge in several weeks.

⁓

Such work does not have to be deliberate or conscious. I have no idea what guides the salmon, beaver, or worm to their work. But I do realize that if the work, in some way, can loop back up "above" the species in a way that alters the flows of energy or resources flowing toward that species, a spiral of cause and effect is created. These feedback loops are the heart of the strategy. They possess unpredictable powers to summon forth rewards and allies within the ecosystem of that species.

We humans possess such an incredible mix of gifts for mastering this strategy. We are mobile consciousness with eyes to see and minds to understand the flows that shape each spot. We have opposable thumbs and tools to interact uniquely yet powerfully with each flow. We have voice and song that allow us to bring our thoughts and actions into resonance with others. We should be able to pass the test with flying colors.

Passing the test does require work. Trees resist the wind. Salmon swim upstream. I am descended from a billion generations that have passed the test. I have inherited their genetic legacy. Perhaps every cell is imprinted with an ancient work ethic. Perhaps I feel the sense of Fit is because my actions fit with a direction coded into my DNA a billion years ago.

An Unexpected Ally

I WAS WAITING IN a checkout line at the grocery store, surrounded by candy bars and tabloid headlines of celebrities divorcing and Elvis reincarnating—a familiar, not very uplifting place to spend time. But that was all right; my mind was elsewhere. I was thinking about the fields, wishing the joyful work they offered me was not restricted to winter storms so that I could do it all the time. And somehow that led back to the question, "What could I do right now to shift a balance toward the upward direction?" I looked around with fresh eyes.

The line formed because the inflow of shoppers to the checkout stand was greater than the outflow. Could the relative balance be shifted? I noticed that the checkout clerk spent most of her time turning parcels around to find their price tags. I tried an experiment: I rearranged the items in my shopping cart so all the price tags faced up.

When my turn came, the lady zipped smoothly through my shopping cart without delay. She smiled. "Thank you so much," she said and continued, "I keep meaning to write a letter to Dear Abby to tell her how much faster it would be if everyone did that."

A successful answer to "What could I do right now to shift a balance toward the upward direction?" encourages me to ask this question more often. In the midst of a conversation outdoors, I noticed the other person squinting. He was facing into the Sun. Squinting drains energy. Yet trading places would only switch who was squinting. What could I do? Asking the question led to the answer. I moved to the side of the person who naturally turned as he talked. Now the Sun was to our side. Neither of us had to squint.

When the healing fields created a shift in my spirit from cynicism to optimism, I realized that this work was healing me as much as it was healing the fields. My continual surprise at the unexpected ways the fields nourish more possibilities should perhaps have signaled me that my healing might also continue in deeper, unexpected ways.

One day I noticed how much energy I was spending trying to second-guess somebody who was untrustworthy. "What a waste," I thought and suddenly, wham, a powerful desire existed within me to be trustworthy so that others, when dealing with me, wouldn't have to waste their energy like this. That desire has never left me since that day (though I'm still working to fulfill it). I find myself trying to do unto others as I would want them to do unto me. I find myself acting more in accordance with basic ethical principles.

I have grown up within a culture where the objective principles of science are presented as free of moral value, the doctrines of religions are seen as subjective, and the law is shaped increasingly by economic interests. In this cultural landscape, ethics wanders homeless. It was hard for me, growing up, to feel a cultural resonance around a sense of direction by which to guide my life. Advertisements urged me to use my energy to consume. I heard lip service given to the work ethic, but I also noticed that work was usually valued for the income it produced rather than the possibilities it created. The goal of work seemed to be to retire comfortably from work as soon as possible. This contradiction left me searching. To accumulate money was the most consistent message I received.

As I grew older, I accepted the culturally sophisticated attitude that morality is relative and that whatever one does is all right as long as it does not hurt anyone. That attitude contains a weak injunction against some negative acts but it provides no inspiration to strive for something. Not until I fell in love with a canyon and tried to shift balances toward the upward direction did I grow beyond that bland morality.

During this work, I watched raindrops hitting the soil. On impact, a raindrop throws soil particles equally in all directions. On a flat slope, just as many particles are thrown just as far in one direction as in the

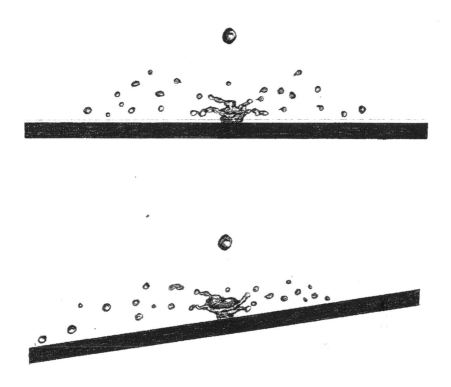

A raindrop throws the same amount of material in all directions. But on a slope, soil thrown downslope travels farther than soil thrown upslope.

opposite direction. The effects of the raindrops cancel one another out. There is no overall movement of the soil.

But on a slope, the soil particles randomly thrown downslope go farther than those thrown upslope. Therefore, the impacts of raindrops do not cancel one another out; the net effect is movement of soil downslope. This accumulative movement is not because of the raindrops—their effect is random, equal in all directions—but because gravity and the slope shape the raindrops' actions.

Images of these splashing raindrops soak into my spirit. The Second Law describes a "slope" to the universe, a direction along which things move more easily one way than the other. If the universe was "flat," I might get away with living a life of random actions without changing the world. But the slope of the universe shapes the impacts of my actions. If I live a life of random actions, I will, through simple chance, tend to move the world downslope.

When I hike in the mountains, the steepness of the slope I walk across is always changing. Sometimes, I walk easily across a level meadow. Sometimes, a foot-wide trail ascends a slope that summons forth deep breathing and steady pacing. And sometimes I cross boulder fields, steep slopes of tippy rocks lying at their angle of repose. Then I am very sensitive to the force of gravity. I am very aware of how easy it is to set rocks bounding down the slope. Precision of weight placement shapes each step across this slope. All my mind is focused. I strive to pass without displacing the tiniest rock. Often, I become so aligned with gravity and the rock I stand upon that lightness and grace emerge. I dance upon a rock. I delight in my ability to move upward in a region so poised to tumble downward.

Just as gravity determines down and up, so the Second Law gives me directions I call "downward" (symbolized by eroding fields) and "upward" (symbolized by healing fields). The Second Law does to my life path what a steepening slope does to my walking. The Second Law heightens my awareness of the possible consequences that reside in every thought, word, and action. When I toss off a put-down of someone, I notice their spirit retract and notice how many minutes of extra effort it takes to restore the relationship to the level before the put-down. Put-downs feel like slips downslope; I try to step more gracefully. Though it is easy to set rocks tumbling down, it's also possible to dance lightly upward.

Each day is filled with a million moves upon the slopes of the Second Law. Any move upon these slopes can remind me of the upward and downward directions. This sense of direction is important. Without a sense of direction, for example, the power of a bomb appears greater than the power of a grass blade. But with a sense of direction, I see that the power of a grass blade is greater in the same way that the number "one" is greater than the number "negative one million."

As I try to align more of my actions to the upward direction, my actions become less random. My life accumulates shape and power. Before my work in Sand Canyon and the fields, I was not able to make the kind of commitment that can carry a couple through the hard times of their relationship. I was not able to sustain the discipline to write the nature stories that were accumulating within me. The Second Law, once a burdensome source of despair, has unexpectedly become an ally of disciplined hope.

The Learning Curve

MY TWO-YEAR OLD daughter and I were playing with large, cardboard blocks. I would line them up and she would mess them up. I would stand a block upright and she would knock it down. The moment I created any order with the blocks, she would disorder them with a laughter that grew almost fiendish in its delight at relentlessly destroying everything.

But then I suddenly saw her actions from a different point of view. My daughter had ignored these blocks until now because she was not strong enough or coordinated enough or precise enough to build anything with them. Since she couldn't do anything interesting with the blocks, they had not been of interest to her. Until now . . .

By setting up blocks in higher energy states, I had created a situation in which her uncoordinated weakness could visibly cause quick, significant changes. By knocking them down, she was discovering that she had the power to change the blocks. Suddenly the blocks were interesting. Now she will begin to play with them. Now she will begin to develop the precision to create patterns, the strength to stack, the perseverance to build towers. The "fiendish" knocking down of blocks was a necessary first step in learning how to build them up.

Children often feel powerless, unable to hammer in a nail or pick up the basket of wet laundry, unable to accomplish most of the Big Wonderful Things that adults do easily all around them. Kids long for a sense of power. I've watched kids work for hours to dislodge a huge boulder on a slope in order to watch it go crashing down. A big movement like this is accessible to them only because its large potential energy is poised on a brink. If it can be tipped just enough, gravity will send it booming down to a lower energy state. Because kids are attracted to big changes, they can sniff out places rich with potential energy just waiting for their interaction to create a big change. As a result, kids' first interactions with a new situation tend to degrade that situation. The Second Law shapes a learning curve in which destruction tends to precede creation.

⌒

Our species is following a similar learning curve in relation to our environment. As a species, we are recently arrived toddlers, knocking down blocks that previous generations of lives have carefully stacked over billions of years. Never in the history of the Earth has a species emerged with such a concentrated power to change the global environment so quickly. The rate at which we use up every source of potential energy we can find is heart-rending. We are in a very dangerous part of a necessary learning curve. By degrading our environment, we are learning that we have the power to change it. Now we can begin to wonder what change in the other (harder) direction would look like. Now we can begin to practice patience, perseverance, and self-restraint. We can learn to listen and watch. If we can learn quickly enough, our current destruction of other species and habitats contains within it a seed of hope.

The Downward Spiral

I SIT IN THE FLOWER-FILLED FIELDS of spring, contented. A marsh hawk glides low over the cattails. Meadowlarks flute from the fenceposts. The swoops of swallows contour the slopes. Grasses colonize the healing gullies. I feel part of a world growing toward unimaginable possibilities. Its loveliness is the accumulative result of life's work over thousands of millions of years. How beautiful life would be if we knew that our grandchildren will live within an even lovelier world with opportunities to nourish possibilities that we cannot even imagine.

Yet when I look beyond these fields I see acres of land disappearing under pavement in the space of a few months. I hear the roar of a freeway even though it is more than a mile away. The freeway throbs day after day, pausing only for Easter morning and Christmas. Thick smog often fills the air. A steady stream of giant garbage trucks grind up the hill behind me to the county dump. The dump is full, but nobody wants a new dump located in his community, so the current landfill grows higher. Across the valley, two military bases sprawl. Convoys of helicopters pass back and forth overhead. Jets blast into the sky, turn, and roar out toward the ocean.

When I journey out of the city, I see gradients of urbanization extending out toward the wild lands. Malls cover the fields. Asphalt storm drains divert the rain, flushing the gift of fresh water back to the sea. Steep-walled gullies grow on overgrazed land. We have deforested the mountains. Seven hundred miles away, we are strip-mining the mesa next to my cliff dwellings for coal to power the lights of city. Gradients of harvesting separate the lands of Gaia's upward spirals from the growing cities. Increasingly, we are surrounded by land that we are draining of its possibilities. No longer can we easily see land in which life creates possibilities. This makes it easy for our urban culture to make a mistake similar to my own with the sand fleas. We assume that it is in the nature of the land to run down.

These gradients of harvesting that surround us remind me of the beaver that were so abundant in the Rocky Mountains two hundred years ago. Geological evidence now reveals how strongly the beaver altered the flow of water and the deposition of soil throughout the mountains and the adjoining prairies. Their dams held together a vast, highly productive hydrologic region. The first Europeans into this region were the mountain men, beaver trappers. They virtually eliminated beaver from this region. Unrepaired dams in trapped-out ponds washed away and the whole hydrologic region unraveled within a few years. The first settlers saw an area already spiraling down and so never realized that it could spiral upward. We who came later never saw how it could be. We lost contact with the ways of Gaia.

Our connection with the land dwindles to a marketing system that provides energy, materials, and food for a price. For most of us, the flow of money seems essential for the sustaining of life. This can lead us to forage for the highest financial rates of return. Unfortunately, if high rate of return becomes the only consideration, then it becomes easy to invest in ventures that cut and run. Though such an approach is profitable for only a little while, the money can then be shifted to another similar venture. Strategies focused exclusively on high rates of return, if successful, will produce high rates of return. Those successfully pursuing such strategies will acquire wealth faster than everybody else. They can use this wealth to increase their cultural power enough to allow them to apply the same strategy to exploit other resources.

It is easy to start on the path of taking too much because the rewards are immediate and any sacrifices seem anonymous and inconsequential. The more we harvest, the more we think we will have. Unfortunately, this is true only in the short run. The living things we harvest are more than just resources for us. They also do Gaia's work. They maintain balances that sustain the environment. If we harvest too much, relative balances shift and the environment begins to slip. Soil erosion increases. Flash floods hit areas downstream of clear-cutting or asphalting. Salmon runs decline. Aquifers decline. The chemical composition of our atmosphere changes.

These diminishing possibilities are warnings. However, if a culture has lost touch with life's power to increase possibilities, then the slipping away of possibilities can tempt people to "get it while the getting is good," to "get it before it is too late," because "if I don't get it, someone else will." We are tempted to act like the people I met who were picking blackberries before they were ripe. The berries were bitterly tart, but if the people waited until the berries were ripe, somebody else might pick the berries first. Now nobody gets to taste a ripe blackberry.

Such behavior creates a spiral. A world that is diminishing in possibilities increasingly appears to justify trying to get enough before it is too late. People who take more than they give are seen as smart; their behavior is imitated. More people try to harvest more than they need. Tragically, the depletion of the Earth seems to justify the very behaviors that are depleting the Earth.

I am saddened by this strategy of building ourselves up by taking too much from the world, because the Second Law of Thermodynamics guarantees that it will run the world down. Maintaining our position with this strategy grows more and more difficult. Contaminated water requires increasingly complex purification processes. Energy exploration requires more energy as the search moves into deeper water and colder lands. Declining aquifers require wells to be drilled deeper and more energy to pump the water up. Fishing nets are made bigger and bigger and require bigger boats to deploy them. Maintaining our position requires increasingly more resources, which makes it ever harder to maintain our position. Fear, doubts, and anxiety consume more personal energy.

As this tragic spiral grows visible, one might consider relinquishing the deteriorating path and returning to the work of the upward path. Yet this choice is difficult if one has internalized "not having to work" as a measure of success. The satisfaction of the upward path's work seems bland compared to the binge of consumption. It is easier to hope the binge can be maintained until after one's own comfortable death. I still remember from my National Park days how many elderly visitors made remarks to the effect of "Well, I'm glad I got to have the good life. The world's a mess but I guess that's your problem to solve."

As the world runs down, it becomes harder to see how the world can "run up." Children growing up in neighborhoods where streams flow in fenced, concrete channels never get to see or play with the way that streams and bordering plants create changes in one another. Children in cities look up into the street-light illumined sky and see only the widely scattered first and second magnitude stars and feel less wonder. As the miracle of this Earth becomes less known, the Earth's majesty becomes less capable of nourishing hope and inspiring restraint on our actions. Motivation sinks from "a higher calling" to "the bottom line."

We have been given the ability to participate consciously in the creation of unimagined possibilities. But this downward spiral cuts us off from our inheritance. As resources diminish, more of the greater system must be harvested. As the areas of harvest expand, they draw closer to the areas of benefit. As the discrepancy between the two areas increases, maintaining the border between them requires more energy. Neighborhoods are built with walls and gates. People increasingly think in terms of "us" versus "them." However, each expansion of the harvest area requires sacrificing some segment of the "us" group. Third World countries are pressed to convert the subsistence land of their people to export-producing plantations for their economy. Some members of Congress try to prohibit the listing of any more endangered species. Corporations restructure and lay off workers and mid-level managers. Who will be next? Bonds of friendship and trust are sacrificed as the "us" group gradually consumes itself.

⌒⌒

When I look beyond my field, I see strawberry fields being harvested cheaply, thanks to people living on the other side of the nearby Mexican border—a sharp boundary that the Border Patrol works hard to maintain with roadblocks and vans. I see sunlight-reflecting concrete laid over sunlight-absorbing pastures. I see throbbing helicopter convoys exhaust petroleum as they practice defending "our" sources of petroleum. I sense a dismal downward spiral within my culture. And yet I am aware that others see a golden future. They point to what I see as accumulations of wealth on the group level. Where they see great opportunity and promise, I see a time lag between two levels of resource flow moving in diametrically opposite directions. How do we communicate between the perspectives of the two different levels in order to agree on what is happening?

The Earth can "run up," can accumulate possibilities. I know it can because I have helped the grass colonize the gullies. We can help the soil grow and raise the Earth. But fleets of huge earthmovers scrape away the soil and massive rollers squash the asphalt flat. The power of billions of dollars drives them on. The city is growing so fast and with such momentum that it is painfully clear that these fields will be "developed" within the next few years. (Though ten years after writing this paragraph, the fields are still there.) Whatever possibilities my work has created for life will be covered with asphalt. The swallows will return one spring and find their fields paved. Office buildings and apartments will evict the mustards, blackbirds, and burrowing owls. I want to protect these lives, to nourish them as they have nourished me, but I have only a shovel.

The overwhelming momentum of that downward spiral often crushes my spirit. Reports of population growth, ecological destruction, and economic pressures make my efforts seem idealistically naive. The times are too desperate; the acts of individuals are too insignificant to make a difference. It's easy to lose hope and sink into routines.

Reversing the Spiral

〜

B UT DOWNWARD SPIRALS can be reversed; I've seen it happen in the fields. Reversing a spiral requires work, but it is possible. Each time I walk in the lands of Gaia, her beautiful, upward spirals rekindle my hope. Each time I watch grass growing in a channel or see soil rising over rocks, I seem to hear Gaia whisper:

〜

Begin the work even though you cannot see the path by which this work can lead to your goal. Do not block your power with your current understanding. Evolution is the process by which the impossible becomes possible through small, accumulating changes.

Concentrate on the direction, not the size of the change. Begin the work with actions that seem tinier than necessary but that are small enough to maintain. The rate of change is slow at first, but do not prematurely judge your efforts. Change happens through spirals; the work grows upon itself. As little changes accumulate, they will reinforce one another and make larger changes possible. Gradually, balances will shift. Enemies that block the way will become allies that lead the way. Where and how this happens cannot be predicted.

You do not work alone. Billions of other living things are doing the work. You are part of an invisible power. As it grows, the erosive power will fade. Begin the work.

〜

This strategy helped me accomplish more in the fields than I thought possible. Can an individual use this strategy to help reverse a culture's downward spiral? Can an individual do more than I usually assume? These questions haunt me with possibilities, so I try to look at my culture as if it were an eroding drainage.

As I observe my culture, the image that I encounter over and over again is "convergence." People flow away from rural areas and converge upon the cities. Shoppers flow away from small local stores and converge upon a few, large, national chain stores and fast food franchises. A global agriculture that once spread its nourishing energy over thousands of edible, genetically diverse plant species now converges its efforts upon a few genetic strains of a few crops. The power to lend money converges onto a few, multi-national banks. The power to present images of the world converges upon a few networks and news magazines. Taxes converge upon distant bureaucracies. I fear that as cultural power converges, like run-off, it achieves erosive proportions despite the best intentions of all through whom it flows.

These convergences remind me of eroding gullies and, like gullies, they inspire in me the same impatient desire for enough power to oppose the power flowing within them. The fields, however, have taught me not to try to oppose the power entrenched within gullies. A better strategy is to go upstream until I find a place where shifting a relative balance is within my power. Tiny shifts up there will create opportunities for other shifts. But where is "upstream" within my culture?

I explore an analogy. In a drainage, upstream is where water flows from. Following this flow to its source leads me to where raindrops first touch the ground. There the rain's power is diffused among a billion raindrops. Some of the raindrops soak in to nourish life; others run off and converge into the power of erosion. The relative balance between these two directions determines the health of the drainage.

In a culture, upstream is where the power of action flows from. Following this power to its source leads me to individuals. There the power of action is diffused among a thousand tiny daily choices. Some actions nourish an upward spiral; others flow away toward erosion. The relative balance between these two directions determines the health of a culture and its environment.

When I explore the headwaters of my culture for causes of erosion, I come upon many widespread assumptions: morality is relative; salary

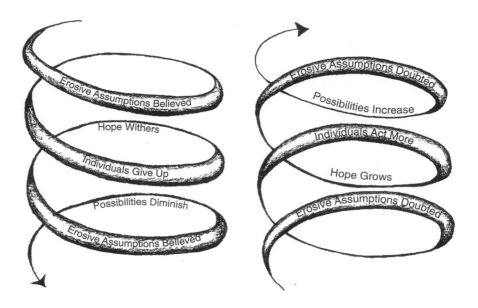

The downward spiral of cultural erosion can reverse to become an upward spiral of cultural healing.

defines a work's worth; all the world is resources for our use; the world is doomed to run down so I might as well "get it before it is too late"; an individual cannot do anything to reverse our downward spiral, so why try. These assumptions cause our personal power to flow away toward cynicism, despair, maintenance of the status quo, thoughtless consumption. As this creative power flows away, people's spirits wither like plants on the terraces above the arroyo.

Shifting those assumptions would help our personal power soak in to nourish hope and inspire individual actions that might help reverse the downward spiral. Helping shift those assumptions feels like something within my personal power. How should I go about it? The fields have taught me to offer new paths rather than simply oppose current paths, and that a series of small divergences is more effective than one large divergence. So I have written this book as a series of tiny divergences, offered to lead you onto new paths of seeing the shadow-rise, watching birds land, noticing grass-clipping dams in street gutters.

Just as my series of little sod divergences reinforced one another and made larger shifts possible, so I hope these little stories will reinforce one another and help you see an environment sustained by life and a world full of flows, balances, and opportunities for shifting those balances. I hope that seeing those opportunities will inspire hope and actions. I hope that this book came to you as a gift and that you pass it on as a gift, so that the giving helps develop and reinforce the networks that bind us into something larger and stronger than we usually realize.

When we see only ourselves, the power within any single action can feel so trivial, especially at first when our actions are tentative. Anything I attempt seems so feeble and apparently has no effect, so why bother? I might as well give up hope and return to routines.

Each action, when seen in isolation, appears as frail as a grass stem buffeted by the prairie wind. The same paradox that hides the wind-absorbing power of the prairie grass or makes invisible the power of Gaia also makes invisible the cultural power of individual actions. This paradox of invisible power can paralyze me psychologically if I am not prepared for it.

However, the smallness that makes individual actions seem insignificant is the very thing that gives them power. Small changes cannot be resisted. Attempts at large changes create large resisting forces but small changes can relentlessly accumulate into significance. Each tiny choice is a tiny source of power.

We are like a prairie whose billion grasses collectively contain the power to slow the run-off, wedge away the wind, and create fertile, rain-absorbing soil. Our individual actions can help Gaia grow. As Gaia grows more visible, more people can see her and feel her invitation to participate consciously in the creation of unknown possibilities. As more people accept this invitation, their nourishing actions will help Gaia grow increasingly visible to still others.

A downward spiral of resignation and apathy can reverse to an upward spiral of invitation and participation. The assumption that "the world is doomed to run down" can shift to the assumption "I can help the world rise toward greater possibilities." The boundary between "us" and "them" can dissolve into a kinship with life. Dreams can grow rather than hopes fade. What can we make possible? Gaia invites us to explore and find out.

Ten Years Later—Going Deeper

*T*HE YOUNG CITY BOYS had never diverged run-off before—but they were enjoying it now. I watched as the oldest
brought a rock to place in a line of rocks that diverted some of the run-
off toward our diversion channel. He was about to put the rock down in
the line when he paused. His eyes moved back and forth along the line of
rocks. Then he placed his rock carefully. I knew exactly what had been
going through his mind, because I have done the same thing a hundred
times. In that moment of empathy, an important meta-lesson arose.

I said, "Triston, I was watching you and I could tell that you were
thinking about which of several places you should place that rock." He
agreed that that had been what he was doing. "What you were doing was
practicing the most important skill you will use in your life. You were
aware that the rock would have different influences depending on where
it was placed and you were deciding which placement would have the
best effect. In life, you will be presented with choices as to where to place
your life energy. You will need to decide which places will create the best
effect on the world around you. So you were practicing with that rock
the same kind of thinking that will help you with your life."

Leading the next generation out into the rain felt so good. Watching
their enthusiastic response to diverging run-off affirmed my enthusiasm.
Alysia and I wanted to create a school where experiences like this could be
part of a child's education. So we created Chrysalis, a chartered public
school with an emphasis on nature study. Many of the ten years since the
self-publishing of the original *Shifting* have been filled with the spiral of
cause and effect that led to Chrysalis. Since that spiral is an example of the
lesson from Gaia—"Begin the work even though you cannot see the path
by which this work can lead to your goal"—I will tell the story.

We didn't start with an idea of a charter school. We were working as teachers for the Carter House Natural Science Museum in very northern California. In presenting a variety of programs, we found that the best responses occurred when students worked with the actual organisms living around them rather than making generic investigations that could be done anywhere in the country. We began to create activities focused on the natural history of our region. The success of these activities led to a five-year grant to create more and teach them as week-long nature investigations in classrooms throughout our region. The enthusiastic response of most students to these investigations led us to wonder what would be possible if, instead of week-long immersions, students had eight years of schooling rich in such investigations.

From this question grew the vision of a chartered public school operating out of our natural science museum. So we went to work to make it a reality. We spent more than a year pushing our proposal and getting nowhere. The administrative and political resistance to a chartered public school (especially one originating outside the system) was enormous. When our latest efforts to meet the annual spring deadline for applications were blocked, we were faced with another year's delay, another year of bureaucratic grinding without any guarantee of success. Was it worth it?

The delight and engagement of our students in the field were so compelling and Alysia's desire to teach so strong, that we would not let our vision be blocked by someone else's power. Instead of seeking permission, we decided to just do it. In the name of research, Alysia persuaded five families to let her teach their children. No money was involved. We had the good will of our museum's director, access to an underused-on-weekdays museum classroom, faith, and eight students. Word gradually spread through the network of mothers, and soon other families asked to join the class. A modest optional tuition evolved to help buy consumables and cover the classroom's utility expenses. By the time the program had grown to fifteen students and been on the local evening news, a local district could see the opportunity and viability of what we were doing and chose to sponsor us as a chartered public school.

Chrysalis now has ninety-five students in kindergarten through eighth grade, and five teachers. We don't intend to grow any larger, because we believe schools should be intimate communities. We walk down to the Sacramento River to watch salmon spawn. We hike to the summits of the surrounding mountains. We sit and watch as thousands of robins gather nightly at their winter roost. We practice seeing cause and effect loops. Our mission is to create a community of learners who mindfully contribute to the upward spirals of the world. We have only achieved a fraction of our vision, but the work is good and the vision deepens.

We hope to help move public education away from a "one model fits all" approach with its emphasis on national standards and testing, and instead move toward a system that can accommodate a greater diversity of approaches. We hope to help create a system in which teachers have more freedom to teach from their hearts. We hope that results from our specific work create a desire within more families everywhere for their children to spend more time outdoors studying the ways of nature. We hope that because of this work, more people will experience the world as an invitation to nourish upward spirals. May the work grow beyond our imagining.

⌒

In the meantime, I still walk in the rain and diverge run-off. I continue partly because it is good work, partly because it is fun, and partly because it has become a personally powerful form of meditation. Within minutes of starting the walk, my mind is deep within a region of awareness I find very hard to access any other way. My perceptions deepen, because I am reading the stories around me in search of clues for how to interact with the land. My thoughts are strong and grounded. When I'm walking in the rain, shovel in hand, I can more easily sense new connections that elude me at other times.

Often Zephyr and Dawn will come on Rain Walks with Daddy. They have learned to love the world awash, the way raindrops hang on branches, the sound of rushing water, the smell of rain-filled air. They have learned . . . well, let them speak for themselves about what they are learning.

Hi, I am Dawn. I go on Rain Walks with my Dad and my sister Zephyr. She is thirteen going on fourteen. I am ten. One of the things I learn on Rain Walks is how streams and brooks can change in the space of one to three months. For example, I have been looking at a stream for about two years now. I can tell you that it changed about three times each year, so I have seen it change six times. Now, that may not seem a lot of times, but if you look on nature's side, that's a lot of change for one stream.

When a stream changes its course, that's when a stream changes shape. One year, I went out and the stream that I named M.N.S. (Mother Nature's Stream) was running straight. Then I came out four weeks later and M.N.S. at one place was going off to the left on a different path. The old path was totally dried up but for a bit of mud. It does that three times a year. As I said, that may not seem a lot, but nature has a lot of things to do. Why don't you try marking a stream? Watch it move and change.

⌒

I'm Zephyr. My name means "a gentle summer breeze." I would like to tell you about a revelation that I had. It was a slightly cloudy day with a light breeze. I saw a hawk riding the thermals that were coming up off the cliffs. She was obviously looking for something, maybe food or a nesting place. She was sticking to her quest but having fun playing in the wind too. Later, when it had started to rain and the wind was strong, I saw the same hawk again. She was still looking for something, and was forced to handle whatever trouble the storm was giving her. Sometimes the wind and rain were so fierce that she could not make any progress. She would just hang there in the air. Other times she would get tumbled and tossed around by the wind. Once I saw her almost get smashed into a tree, but she pulled out at the last moment. I started to think about how like ourselves she was. She was trying to accomplish something and she was not letting the storm discourage her. But most importantly, she was handling it with grace and determination. Even when it was so bad that she could not do anything, she would just wait until things got better and then continue. Just before the wind smashed her into the tree, she pulled it together, took control of herself, and turned at the last moment. I began to think of the winds as fate and of the hawk as myself. Later, when the winds had diminished, I saw her again. She was building a nest high in an oak. When she flew out for sticks she would play on the thermals. As I watched her, I realized that I am in control. If I have the strength, determination, and courage to defy the wind and stick it out, the rewards will come. Since watching that hawk, I have pulled myself out of several problems in my life with what I hoped was grace. The rewards have come. I can go through life feeling a little lighter. I learned this lesson simply by watching a determined hawk. Just think what this world would be like if everyone watched and learned from the animals.

⌒

Walking with my daughters is an unpredictable delight. Another unpredictable delight is discovering the ways the land responds to our work. Willow cuttings placed in a large streambed, for example, have grown and baffled the current. This slowing of the water created a deposit of gravel across the streambed that is twenty feet long but only a few inches high. This almost invisible dam creates a long quiet stretch of water upstream with a sandy bottom, which now brings forth many more milkweeds in the summer, which nourish many more caterpillars of the brilliant Monarch butterflies. Meanwhile, on a hillside, our diversion of water around a system of gullies has led to a gopher-powered soil cycling that fills in small gullies in the most head-scratching, fascinating way.

The work has grown beyond the diverging of run-off. I'm experimenting now with strategically fertilizing rocky, ephemeral streambeds to help plants get established in this difficult-to-colonize habitat. I'm learning how to time and place my mowings in order to favor the native perennial grasses in the grasslands around me.

⌒

Another unpredictable, satisfying area of growth over the last ten years has been what I've learned from readers who have written to me in response to the first edition of this book. One particular area of growth has come about thanks to those readers whose deepest response was to the structure of the book. The structure was shaped by a rule: Stories First. Whatever philosophy I wanted to present had to come after (and hopefully arise spontaneously from) the stories. I knew this rule was important, though I could not articulate why. However, readers made comments and shared articles that helped me understand the beneath-the-words message conveyed by this structure. Thanks to those readers, I think I can now (ten years later) lift that structural message up to the level of words. But I'll start with a story.

I was teaching a fifth-grade class how to see through time by having each student arrange the different stages of a plant's flowering into a sequence so they could see the process by which it developed over time. One boy just couldn't get it. A gap in the middle of his buttercup sequence prevented his mind from flowing all the way from flower bud to seeds. I found an example of the intermediate stage that fit into the gap. He studied the sequence for a few seconds and then an expression of spontaneous, pure delight burst forth. "Ooh. That's cool!"

Now let me follow that story with an analogy. Whenever my foot "falls asleep," walking feels awkward. I clomp about. This awkwardness is not because the muscles have fallen asleep. The muscles are working just fine and, theoretically, I am capable of moving my "asleep" foot with just as much grace as when my foot is awake. What has fallen asleep are the nerves that send feedback on the position of my foot. Walking is a spiral of storytelling between my foot and brain. My brain tells my foot what to do and my foot tells my brain what the foot is actually doing. When my foot falls asleep, my brain can't hear the story that the foot is telling. Without that feedback, I move awkwardly. As the nerves "wake up" and my brain starts to hear the story again, I move with increasing grace.

Life is a spiral of storytelling between my actions and the world. My book is a series of stories about times when I "woke up" and heard a story the world was telling that increased my awareness of what I was actually doing within this universe. ("Ooh, the horizon's rising. That's cool.") This feedback allows me to live with greater grace. This increasing grace is what the words in this book tell about.

If I was cynical, I would say that, as a culture, our "feet" have fallen asleep and we are clomping about. And there is some temporary truth in that, what with the hypnotic chattering of advertising, the mesmerizing flickering of television and computer screens, the monotone sound of traffic, the uniformity of asphalt underfoot and roofs overhead. But I prefer to think that I have been born into the midst of the Earth "waking up" over billions of years and that my being alive can contribute to that process of waking up.

The world is alive with stories; wisdom is whispered to us continuously, wisdom that can guide our lives into upward spirals if we learn to listen. But the wisdom is not whispered in words. (We use words afterward to hold onto that wisdom.) The wisdom comes more viscerally, like the spontaneous burst of joy from the boy seeing the buttercup sequence for the first time, and it comes through one specific encounter at a time. This is the message embedded in the book's structure. The structure of "stories first" works because learning springs from specific encounters.

This message of structure combines with the message of words to say that listening to the world can stir emotions that can guide our lives into upward spirals of grace. This is an amazing thing: The non-verbal, unconscious world can somehow grace our lives with wisdom. The implication is that the world is more than our culture imagines and that we fit within this world in a far deeper way than we usually explore. Let me share one last story from the edge of my first explorations.

A half-year after graduating from college, I was lost. I had believed all the messages proclaiming that the key to success was a college education. I had followed those instructions, gotten my degree, and now had no idea what I was supposed to do with my life. Living at home and helping Dad with his business gave some healthy structure to what otherwise might have been a very dangerous time. I poured an addictive amount of money into pinball machines. I spun dispiritedly in an eddy. One day I noticed that for weeks I had been practicing driving faster and faster on winter mountain roads. Was I unconsciously trying to kill myself? That realization focused me on "What do I really want to do?" Not on a cosmic level, which had stymied me, but on a small level of "what's some activity I've always wanted to do?"

The first thing that came to mind was climbing to the top of the thousand-foot high cliffs that border the highway thirty miles from my hometown in southeastern Washington. Every time we had driven that highway during my childhood, I had gazed up at those basalt cliffs and wondered what was on top. And so, one day during my post-college darkness, I parked amidst the sagebrush and started to climb. A side valley led me behind the cliffs. Small alcoves of intimate beauty nestled within the contours of this steep, arid, lovely land. Ascending the valley led me to the vast rolling scrubland on top. From there I walked out to the edge. The grass-covered soil thinned to bedrock.

The cliff edge was sheer, dropping several hundred feet to talus slopes that slanted the rest of the thousand feet. I gazed out over many miles of land that I had driven through for years but never seen from this perspective. Eventually my attention drew closer to the cliff itself. The cliff was not smooth like granite or sandstone but was a sheer mosaic of tiny ledges, crannies, and nubbins caused by the erosion of cooled basalt. After many minutes, my eyes noticed a flitting motion on the cliff walls a hundred feet away. It looked as if the ledges and nubbins were rearranging themselves. As this sphere of rearranging energy gradually moved closer, it resolved into a flock of small birds the rich color of the brown basalt. They were foraging for seeds upon the cliff itself, fluttering from one tiny ledge to another.

I lay on my belly and hung my head over the edge for a closer view. Soon they were close enough for me to study them individually. Strange little birds—brown with gray heads, but when they fluttered, I saw— pink? Such an exotic bird mundanely foraging in such a spectacular place. They would encounter little competition on these unreachable tiny ledges.

One of them landed on a ledge just a few feet below me. I watched as it searched about for wind-tossed seeds. All my attention became absorbed in the few-inch world of this ledge and this individual bird. The few flakes of basalt that had fallen onto the ledge huddled away from the edge and the great void beyond. The bird's head kept turning so that an eye could look up at me or look down for seeds, look out for prairie falcons, look over at others in the flock. Pinkish feathers occasionally peeked out from beneath brown feathers. With wings completely closed, the bird casually hopped off the ledge and dropped from sight. Without warning. Something moved in my belly.

I hiked down the slope without the depression I had carried up. I was out of my eddy and back in the current of life. Fascination with that bird led me to buy a field guide. Reading the guide allowed me to identify the bird as a grey-crowned rosy finch, but it also got me interested in birdwatching. Birdwatching quickly got me traveling around the West all spring to see different birds in different habitats. Several birdwatchers said I had to experience Alaska in the summer, so I hitchhiked up there. While spending a month in Denali National Park, I watched a great ranger, William Rodamor, give a great campfire program. Suddenly I knew what I wanted to do with my life: be a ranger giving campfire programs in Denali National Park. I achieved that goal four years later and by that time, my life path was self-sustaining.

But what happened on that clifftop? What I think happened was that the bird showed me what faith in life looks like. Without even looking down first, the bird simply hopped off the edge, wings folded, because it was sure it could fly. Something in my belly responded and followed, hopping off the ledge I had been clinging to fearfully. But this explanation came days afterward. If the explanation is true, the communication had nothing to do with words or thoughts; it was much more direct. The bird hopped off, something in my belly moved in immediate response—and the depression was gone. I was back in the flow of life.

A small bird has the power to alter my life by moving some powerful part of me that our culture doesn't even talk about. This is the world we truly live in; one that can alter our lives with the drop of a bird. Mystery fills this world.

That bird is more than a bird. That bird has survived early summer snowstorms at timberline. That bird has been lifted skyward by great updrafts of energy within the air. Millions of generations of its ancient ancestors have flown out over open ocean, betting their lives that land will be where their instinct tells them it will be.

That cliff is more than a cliff. It was stripped by the cataclysmic floods from Lake Missoula. It has received thousands of years of bird droppings vibrating with Columbia River salmon energy. That cliff towered above Lewis and Clark's boats. It felt the eternal flow of the mighty Columbia River come to a halt following the construction of McNary Dam.

And I am more than a person. I am one of a recently evolved species. We are mobile consciousness, gifted with incredible powers: powerful vision to see what needs to be done; opposable thumbs so we can do the work with a variety of powerful tools; and voices so we can bring our actions in resonance with one another and then pray and sing as we work together.

We live within a world thick with relationships chanting stories. Even so, I can forget to listen. Then my awareness ebbs. I start thinking of myself as separate, alone, autonomous—like a tidepool drying out, abandoned by the receding tide. I slip into routines and inspiration slips away. I clomp around with a spirit that has "fallen asleep." But when I listen to the stories that the world tells, the inspiration and the power return (like waves to the tidepool) and my life takes on grace.

We are like soil, the creation of millions of lives that preceded us, upon which a great mysterious rain falls. Like the soil, whatever we can absorb from that rain has the power to expand us, transform us. Like an earthworm within the soil, may these sharings help open you to the mysterious rain of power that falls upon this Earth. May new possibilities grow from the soil of our spirits.

Acknowledgments

⌒

*T*HREE BOOKS GUIDED ME into the wilderness.

Colin Fletcher's *The Complete Walker* (since revised to *The Complete Walker III*, Alfred A. Knopf, Inc., 1984) inspired me to backpack solo at the same time it gave me enough information to feel comfortable doing so. The information on equipment might be outdated but the zesty joy within this book still radiates.

On the Loose by Terry and Renny Russell (Sierra Club Book, 1969) inspired eager roaming. "Beauty is not on the map. Seek and ye shall find."

Birds of North America (A Golden Field Guide, by Robbins, Brunn, Zim, and Singer. Published by Golden Press, 1966) helped me look at birds, which led me to wanting to see more birds, which required me to visit more habitats, and so off I went.

⌒

Whole Earth Review (formerly *Coevolution Quarterly*) has never failed to stretch and inspire my thoughts in a diversity of unpredictable ways four times a year. Subscriptions are $24 (1999 price) from Whole Earth Customer Service, P.O. Box 3000, Denville, NJ 07834. Many of my thoughts began as seeds that arrived in that magazine. Three major seeds are:

Gary Snyder—I began my years in the Park Service with a quote of his taped to the wall. The quote went something like: "It is best to think of this as a revolution, not of guns, but of consciousness, which will be won by seizing the key myths, archetypes, eschatologies, and ecstasies so that life won't seem worth living unless one is on the transforming energy's side."

General Systems Thinking helped me see the patterns underlying a diversity of situations. I've read enough books on this subject for them to blur together yet every one felt fresh and worthwhile. Go to your library and look under "systems thinking" and see what you find.

And, of course, the Gaia Hypothesis. I first encountered James Lovelock and Lynn Margulis in *Coevolution Quarterly*. The magazine led me to Lovelock's book, *Gaia: A New Look at Life* (Oxford University Press,. 1979).

I am grateful to: the National Park Service for preserving large expanses of wilderness; Michael Butler and his Farm School at U.C.I. for teaching me how to teach (as opposed to lecture); those scientists who developed the science of ecology; the dancers/teachers of Skinner Releasing Ensemble in Seattle for showing me that it is possible; and the grey-crowned rosy finch who started it all.

I bow with respect to Chelsea Green Publishing Company. I was continually caught off-guard by how they asked for my opinion on all aspects of book production (then later was grateful). I honor them for creating sustainable relationships with their authors, distributors, and readers when the publishing industry is being ravaged by the cut-and-run tactics of publishing giants. May Chelsea Green live long and prosper.

In his book, *Design with Nature* (John Wiley and Sons, Inc., 1991), Ian McHarg wrote an amazing essay, "The Naturalists," in which he presents the reverential, upward path he finds in the Second Law. I read it during my time among the cliff dwellings.

For the editorial assistance of helping me see my writing from the perspective of the reader and telling me that the book was still not finished, I thank Jan Gandy, Tobby Brandtman, Bill (my father), and Bill (my brother). Special editorial thanks go to Alysia and Jean Krafel who gave the amount of time one could hope for only from a wife and a mother.

Then there is Rachael Cohen of Chelsea Green, who took a book I'd been comfortable with for ten years and raised it to a higher level. She did this by suggesting changes to tighten the prose but far more impressively, she asked questions and pointed out ambiguities that made me revisit sections at a much deeper level. Much of the new material in this book is a result of her precise probing.

⌐⌐

Finally, in almost every acknowledgment I have ever read, the author thanks his or her family for being supportive through the writing of the book. Now I know why. The process of sharing all aspects of authoring and publishing with my daughters has been a blessing. My wife, Alysia, has given energy in so many ways that this book has become our book. Many of the sentences and paragraphs are hers. She wishes to thank Dr. Adrian Pollack whose patient tutoring helped her understand negative acceleration, a concept that underlies time lags and feedback loops. She especially acknowledges the ideas and powerful teaching of Andrew J. Galambos. It is through the lenses of physics and volition as presented by Galambos that she understood and edited my work.

Author's Invitation

I ENJOY HEARING THE UNIQUE INSIGHTS and applications each reader makes in response to *Seeing Nature*. I can't guarantee a reply, especially during the school year, but I would enjoy hearing from you. I continue to explore the upward spirals of Gaia and how we can participate within them. Sometimes this work happens out in the wilderness. Sometimes it happens while teaching children. Sometimes it happens in my daily family life.

Several years ago I started a quarterly newsletter to create an external deadline to help discipline me into keeping track of and expressing deeper thoughts. If you would like to receive a copy of *Cairns of HOPE*, send $1.00 (to cover printing, postage, and handling) to Paul Krafel, P.O. Box 609, Cottonwood, CA 96022-0609.

Or you can receive it free by e-mail by sending me a message at:

akrafel@enterprise.k12.ca.us